I0056229

Praise for

Kosher Giving

"Kosher Giving" by Avi Zimmerman provides a valuable resource for everyone engaged in any form of philanthropy. I believe that more money is wasted by well meaning philanthropists who do not adopt the principles of meaningful, mindful, and measurable phil-anthropic investments, which they actually do when making for profit investments. Mr. Zimmerman provides an excellent roadmap to giving meaningfully and strategically, which results in giving effectively. The references to Torah and Maimonides wonderfully demonstrate why and how our Jewish tradition teaches us to make this world better than we found it through joyful/proactive/strategic giving —both of ourselves and our resources. "Kosher Giving" is a great guide for both new and veteran philanthropists.

—**Richard Sandler,** Executive Vice President and Trustee of Milken Family Foundation Past Chairman of the Board of Jewish Federations

I read your book and found it a powerful reminder of how we should act, not just in times of struggle, but at all times. As you indicated early in your introduction, "This book is for anyone and everyone who has asked themselves, 'What can I do to fix things?' 'What's my role?' or 'What's my purpose?' The book is not simply about philanthropy...it is a primer on how each of us can live a life of significance. If we follow the precepts that form the foundation of Kosher Giving, we can make a difference and, more importantly, walk with our G-d!

—**General Charles C. Krulak,** 31st Commandant of the US Marine Corps Former Member of the Joint Chiefs of Staff

October 7th marked a hinge of history for Israel and the Jewish people. It also marked an unprecedented opportunity for Christians to stand with their Jewish brothers and sisters in their darkest hour since the Holocaust. In Kosher Giving my friend Avi Zimmerman lays out a clear, succinct and impassioned plan for giving to Israel "for such a time as this!"

—**Chris Mitchell,** Christian Broadcast Network

Great read, timeless and sound guidance. In the midst of the Iron Swords War, Avi Zimmerman has written a compelling guide illustrating how and why to support Israel. His work examines the larger question, "Why give to Israel?" Among his solid conclusions the reader finds inspiring thoughts about giving because much has been given by God to us. Avi lives his life with the promises of God for Israel and her people foremost in his heart and mind.

—**Richard Stimpson,** Chairman and Investment Counselor
Leavell Investments

In Kosher Giving, Avi encourages and empowers the giver to be not just a source but also a steward of the blessings they seek to confer. As I read through the book, I couldn't help but consider how many of these principles apply to investing as well. Giving, really, is investing in a cosmic, kingdom of heaven sort of way. Bringing Biblical wisdom and the wisdom of the Jewish sages to bear on the topic makes this a timeless, thought-provoking read!

—**Marcus D Bowman, CPA, CEPA,** Principal CliftonLarson- Allen LLP

As philanthropy has matured over the past decades, many donors are no longer satisfied with simply giving. Rather, they want to be sure that their gift makes a real difference to those in need. Kosher Giving provides these donors with a clear and concise approach to enhancing their philanthropy, encapsulated in the book's three pillars of Meaningful, Mindful, and Manifest giving. Applied properly, this approach can ensure that our giving achieves the powerful impact which donors seek, and which recipients so desperately need.

—**Rabbi Dr. Barry Kislowicz,** Senior Director, Scott Goldberg Consulting

Having worked with Avi on the ground for impact investment assessment I know he is as pragmatic as he's thoughtful. I find the three pillars of Kosher Giving: meaningful, mindful and measurable aligned with my own practice of Biblical stewardship and portfolio driven generosity. This practical guide is not just for the wealthy philanthropist but for everyone who wants to be faithful stewards.

—**David Lin,** Microsoft Venture Accelerator China founder
Author, Speaker and Executive Coach

Charity is so built into the Jewish DNA, that we don't always think about it deeply or strategically. I am therefore so grateful for Avi Zimmerman's phenomenal new book, "Kosher Giving" for offering thoughtful insights into how our charity can be more meaningful and impactful. Especially now, when Israel and the Jewish people are in crisis and at a crossroads, Avi Zimmerman's "Kosher Giving" should be read by everyone who wants to ensure that our philanthropic resources are best utilized to ensure a better future.

—**Rabbi Tuly Weisz,** Founder of Israel365 and Editor of "The Israel Bible"

You can tell who your true friends are in times of greatest need. As Israel's [...] enemies gather at its borders and global antiSemitism rises to unprecedented levels, the world's one and only Jewish State is in need of faithful friends who can help bolster its continued security, prosperity and way of life. With Kosher Giving, my friend Avi Zimmerman draws on his years of experience on the ground, in the trenches and in boardrooms worldwide to lay out the definitive blueprint for lovers of Zion who desire to help Israel not only survive but thrive.

—**Erick Stakelbeck,** TBN News Director and Host of The Watchman

Avi's approach in Kosher Giving is very fitting - he is willing to bring to light the hidden and challenging areas of giving while providing clarity to the "why" and "where". Thoughtful questions and action steps throughout the book will help you grow in your giving!

—**Brad Formsma**, Best selling author of "I Like Giving" and
The WOW Factor podcast

Kosher Giving written by my dear friend, Avi Zimmerman was birthed during a tragedy. On October 7, 2023, the brutal attack on Israel by Hamas awakened the world to see the sheer hatred behind anti-Semitism that the Jewish people have experienced for several centuries. During World War II, sadly, the Church was largely silent during the Holocaust. As Jews emerged from the Shoah and made Aliyah to the new State of Israel, their battle cry was "Never again!" For many of us who are Evangelicals, "Never again!" has be-come our battle cry as well.

Since October 7th, Israel has experienced a wave of stunning generosity and I'm happy to say the Church has not held back. That's why I'm thrilled with Avi's new book-Kosher Giving! Avi so eloquently underscores the need for Kosher Giving this way: Philanthropy requires more than just meaningful commitment. It demands a mindful approach to resource allocations. Amen Avi!

I loved this book and talk about timely! The mindful approach you laid out in Kosher Giving comes from the Bible and years of successful, entrepreneurial leadership. Thank you for sharing it with us! As a pastor and the CEO of a non-profit organization, I resonated with this purposeful plan for giving that provides the tools to chart your course through the maze of giving opportunities available today. No one wants to give generously and end up wasting the resources God has blessed them with. Kosher Giving will give you a plan to avoid the trap of giving to something that sounds good but ends up amounting to nothing. There is a strategy and Avi has laid it out for you to follow with ease.

—**Tom Doyle CEO,** Uncharted Ministries Best-Selling Author of multiple titles including "Two Nations Under God-Why YOU Should Care About Israel"

Kosher Giving

4 Steps to a Meaningful, Mindful and Measurable Philanthropy Plan

Avi Zimmerman

Beverly House Press

Published by Beverly House Press

Beverly House Press books are available at special discounts for bulk purchases in the United States by corporations, institutions, and other organizations. For more information, please contact markets@beverlyhousepress.com.

Published by Beverly House Press
304 E. Pine St. #1058
Lakeland, FL 33801

www.BeverlyHousePress.com

Library of Congress Control Number: 2024901060

ISBN: 978-1-957466-06-4 (Hardback)

To Brant, Sally, Vann, Crawford and William Grier.

Thank you for Shalom Giving.

Contents

Foreword

The basketball players at Auburn will tell you that I expect and respect personal values, on and off the court.

Our values are the backbone to our sportsmanship, and the backbone to our success and our culture. If you know what you stand for then you will know how to perform. But what happens when there are conflicting values? What happens when we are influenced to conduct ourselves one way on the court, and another way off the court? How can we get the many moving parts of our personality and our team to sync up? These questions can be especially challenging when dealing with your people.

The answer is that we need a strategy. Every value needs a home, a context, a plan, and an opportunity to be fully expressed. In this case, what is true for effective, purpose-driven basketball is true for effective, purpose-driven philanthropy.

Four years ago, I began developing an appreciation for strategic philanthropy and the impact that it generates for donors and beneficiaries alike. I had witnessed the ins and outs of fundraising for most of my career, and I had just joined the U.S. Israel Education Association (USIEA) on a life-changing fundraising trip to Israel.

It was on this trip that I met Avi Zimmerman. Avi was on the founding Board of Directors for USIEA and has greatly impacted the organization's growth for over a decade.

Avi had applied an innovative approach that would impact the value-add for giving within USIEA. He was all about punching above your weight class through strategic planning with compelling outcomes well beyond a dollar-for-dollar return on philanthropic investment.

Later, when I also assumed a Board role at USIEA, we were invited to develop tools for the U.S. Congress to make better informed decisions about U.S. policy regarding Israel. With USIEA providing a deep-dive on the issues and developing high-impact delegations for senior members of Congress to the region, donors could have the confidence that their contributions would be directed not only to a specific set of outcomes, but also towards policy that will influence a broad landscape of opportunities.

Of course, this work is not simple. It requires a sensitivity to international diplomacy, an appreciation for the roles and limitations of a nonprofit entity, and clearly articulated goals and objectives. Even more demanding, it rests upon a rich value system, marked by uncompromising integrity and mutual respect. Fortunately, Avi made himself available to walk us through these processes.

Very few groups visiting Israel venture into Judea and Samaria, commonly known as the West Bank. For those who do, they tend to exclusively visit either the Israeli or Palestinian communities. But with Avi as our host, we can engage with both and see a more complete vision of the modern Israel-Palestinian dynamic in the communities and the philanthropies that support them.

Whether it's a Congressional delegation or a group of philanthropists, USIEA always spends two tour days with Avi. One day is committed to Ariel, seeing Israelis and Palestinians working side by side in industrial parks, experiencing the Ariel National Leadership Center, and learning about the revolutionary Ariel University. Another day is spent with Avi in Hebron, visiting with our friend Sheikh Ashraf Jabari and meeting Palestinian members of the Judea and Samaria Chamber of Commerce and Industry which Ashraf and Avi lead voluntarily together. These two days in the West Bank with Avi are extremely unique and essential to understanding the region. Any trip would be incomplete without including both on the itinerary.

I'm excited to see that the work that I have done with Avi is now available to a broad audience via the pages of this book. Through his appreciation for a broad range of values, each of which he lives out, and his experience with strategic planning for both nonprofits and donors, Avi introduces us to a way to create a dynamic giving plan based on his Kosher Giving paradigm.

By systematically unpacking the philanthropist's journey into pillars, phases, and partnerships, Kosher Giving becomes more than a playbook; it's a full framework for how we, as donors, move from giving because 'we care' to giving as a core element of our life's purpose.

The timing of this book could not be more critical. In the weeks and months following the Hamas terror organization's onslaught of Israeli communities on October 7, there has been a groundswell of unprecedented needs, unprecedented civil society initiatives in Israel, and unprecedented support from philanthropists across the globe. But how do we synchronize needs, impact agent-builders, and resources? How can we make giving more impactful? And how can we make impact more purposeful?

The Auburn Tigers would never show up to a game without a strategic plan. The outcome of our competitions means too much to our players, our fans, and of course to me. Basketball means too much to the players and me for us to show up casually. If there are parts of your life such as giving, that you consider meaningful, then I strongly encourage you to take them just as seriously.

In Kosher Giving, Avi challenges us to make a paradigm shift. He challenges us to give better, not by giving more but by giving more thoughtfully. It's a challenge to take the time, commit to a process, develop a plan, implement, learn, and refine. It's a challenge to do philanthropy just as well as anything else that matters to us - with intent, commitment, and dignity. This challenge is a call to action for anyone who gives, and an opportunity for those who want to give better.

Thank you for the invitation, Avi. I accept. To whom much is given, much is expected.

Bruce Pearl
Head Coach
Auburn University Men's Basketball
USIEA Board of Directors

Preface

11 Kislev, 5784 / November 24, 2023

They say that time heals all wounds. Personally, I'd rather not wait.

It's day 49 since the Hamas terror organization's brutal October 7 massacre of Israel's south. Amid the rollercoaster of emotions that have swept over us since the Iron Swords War began, today stands out, infused with a heightened sense of cautious anticipation.

At 4:00 pm Jerusalem time, 50 Israeli women and children who were kidnapped on the "Black Sabbath" and held in captivity ever since are expected to be released, one group at a time. We can't be sure how the exchange with Hamas will play itself out. We don't know what state our extended family members will be in upon their return, and we know even less about most of the captives, whose names were not included among those fortunate enough to be released. Uncertainty, optimism, and mixed emotions abound.

Ironically, this manuscript's deadline coincides with the captives' scheduled release. The Jewish Sabbath, Shabbat, will be upon us, and I will have sent this work to the publishers, by the time they're back on Israeli soil. For me, it's an inflection point.

Israel continues to process the events of the past 7 weeks. On the third day of the war, still numb with disbelief, our Sector4 Strategy team asked ourselves the same question that echoed in the hearts of many: What can we do to help? But it wasn't until our weekly

"Strategic Philanthropy Services" Zoom call that our role in this "new normal" came into focus.

From the beginning, it was obvious that Israel was facing unprecedented challenges. Friends of Israel from around the world were giving more than every before. At the same time, there was a surge in need for volunteers as well as requests to take action across Israel's civil society. This meant that there were more needs to meet, more resources to manage, more people involved, and naturally, more potential inefficiencies than ever before.

There have always been gaps in the giving process, but they grow wider, into chasms, when everything increases in scale. With Israel in a state of fundamental disorder, we had to decide: which of these growing gaps could we most effectively address?

Joey Selesny, an associate and highly skilled professional in the non-profit sector, came forward with an idea. He suggested that our team at Sector4 Strategy invest our time, effort, and resources to provide daily updates on meaningful and reliable initiatives for the international community of donors. After all, a key issue experienced by donors both in Israel and abroad was the challenge to fully grasp the extent of the needs. While it was impossible to cover every need and giving opportunity across the country, we could leverage our networks to identify worthwhile causes, apply our proven methodology to evaluate the projects, and use technology to reach and inform a wide array of philanthropists, beyond our usual client base.

We knew enough about content development to know that daily posts worth reading would require a significant commitment on our part. But what choice did we have? As an Israel-based, purpose-driven, strategic advisory group, we felt obligated to do our best to fill this gap.

Later that evening, we secured the KosherGiving.com domain and started to build what would become a volunteer-driven social impact platform. Web developers, content writers, editors, graphic designers, and social media experts all came together with a shared goal: to make a difference in the philanthropy space. Each person was motivated to apply their skills and make an impact. They wanted to feel they were fulfilling their role and aligning their actions with a higher purpose.

In life, we can be called to act at any given moment. Our goal is to be able to respond with our resources and abilities, and to do so effectively. If you're a soldier on the frontlines, your role is crystal clear. However, when you're a civilian on the home front, the task is not to respond to a call but to proactively identify the call that has your name on it.

This book, much like the KosherGiving.com website, is not designed for Israelis. Despite what the title might suggest (see the Introduction for more details), it's also not limited to the Jewish Diaspora. And even though one of the frames of reference is the current war in this region, the insights offered here are universally relevant. This book is for anyone and everyone who has ever asked themselves "what can I do to make things better?" "What's my role?" or "What's my purpose?" as it relates to their giving and philanthropy.

Yes, Kosher Giving, both the initiative and the concept, is about purpose. It's looking outwards at the needs, inwards at ourselves, and asks how it all syncs up. If giving is how we make a positive impact on the world around us, then kosher giving is about doing it more effectively.

For me, this has been a meaningful opportunity to bring my past 15 years of professional experience as a social and business entrepreneur, working with nonprofits, the private sector, and government. I know that the experiences I've had can help others as they navigate uncertainty and optimism. As such, this serves as a source of purpose and a commitment to playing my part.

Thank you to the exceptional Sector4 Strategy team, and particularly to Jael Kurtz and Avraham Lifshitz, for dedicating countless hours and effort to bring KosherGiving.com to life.

Thank you to Metuka Benjamin, Heather Johnston and Marcus Bauman for answering the call and joining our Advisory Board.

Thank you to Aliyah Schneider and Dr. Barry Kislowicz for your thoughtful contributions on our weekly Editorial Board calls.

Thank you to Tal Mizrachi for building the KosherGiving.com website, despite having to dodge rockets as you commuted to and from our meetings. And thank you to Gitty, Jesse, and Katie for stepping in whenever you were needed. Thanks to Talia Blatman, Kally Kislowicz and, D'vora Klein for heading up copywriting. And thank you to all of the new and future volunteers who have offered their time, services, and talents to this ever-developing process.

Thank you, Yael Maoz and Beverly House Press, for the direction, professionalism, and fresh intensity that you brought to the term 'expedite.'

Thank you to the exceptional individuals who stepped forward to fund this project, some of whom appear on the pages of this book. You heard the call and leaned in; for this, I am extremely appreciative.

And, of course, thank you to Dana, my wife and life partner, for your endless support. These last couple of weeks of writing have been relentless. You've held the fort, silently took care of 80 reservists' families, and hosted daily camps for kids at home, all while keeping to your regular commitments, tending to National Service volunteers in Israel and abroad. I will not begin to speak of your virtues, just in case there are people who read this far into the Preface. Please forgive me for sharing a glimpse at your awe-inspiring and unassuming accomplishments. I am forever grateful.

Thank you to Gilli Shirah, Eytan Ohr, Leebie Tzion, Ari Yisrael, and Noam Eliyah, for giving me the time and space to finish this project. It might not seem like much, but this is my best effort at making a difference.

And thank you, G-d. For everything.
Avi

Who Should Read This Book?

Do you have a generous spirit, a discerning mind, and the funds to make an impact in a world you are proud to inhabit and pass down to future generations?

Are you an organized individual floating in a vast sea of philanthropic data and looking for a stable structure on which to build your approach and a clear guide to achieving your philanthropic goals?

Are you a leader and visionary, tasked with the responsibility of guiding those who have put their trust and fortunes in your hands to make impactful changes during uncertain times?

Are you Jewish, Christian, Agnostic... or a friend to humanity who has faith and hope in a more peaceful and prosperous future for all?

Whether you've always given, are new to giving, want to give more, or want to give differently, if you sense that there's a better way to give, and you want to learn how...

This book is for you.

My Promise

By the time you finish this book, you will have created your own Kosher Giving Plan. This plan will be customized to your personal values, resources, preferred partners, and vision for making an impact.

You will be equipped with the knowledge and tools to effectively identify needs, understand the value of collaborating with different impact partners, and learn to ask the right questions to define you or your organization's purpose in giving.

You'll be motivated by stories of donors and philanthropists who are making positive change in times of war and peace alike, and gain insights into:

- Critical decision-making processes during extreme circumstances and through strategic planning.
- When and how to temporarily or permanently shift focus in response to changing situations.
- The tools and insights you need to assess needs, identify impactful projects, and measure your success.
- How to effectively match resources with specific needs.
- Achieving alignment between good intentions and impactful, measurable outcomes.

You'll be provided a framework for your own Kosher Giving Plan and receive step-by-step guidance through the phases of building and refining your plan, year after year.

You'll understand how giving in times of peace critically differs from crisis philanthropy and how a shift between the two realities can impact your own giving plan.

You'll complete this book a more mindful giver, impactful donor, and purposeful leader.

Introduction to Kosher Giving

Kosher. For many, the term conjures images of ritualistic practices, dietary laws, and religious customs. But this book is not about dietary rules or religious directives. It delves into a broader, universal concept of 'kosher'.

At its core, 'kosher' signifies a way of life and, as explored in this book, a way of giving. It embodies a meaningful, mindful, and measurable approach to our world and our actions within it.

Why Kosher Giving?

'Kosher giving,' a concept rooted in vision and framework, guides us to give thoughtfully and with impact. The word "kosher" originates from the Hebrew term "kasher," meaning "fit" or "proper." Much like in the world of food where kosher signifies purity and adherence to particular standards, we can adapt these principles to our everyday actions, particularly our giving.

For those practicing kosher dietary habits, each meal begins with a crucial question: "Is this kosher?" Eating, an inherently good and necessary act, is approached with mindfulness and adherence to a set of values. This book extends that concept to philanthropy, exploring how giving, although naturally positive and productive, also warrants the question: "Is our giving kosher?" The kosher question prompts us to consider if our giving is meaningful, mindful, and measurable.

Meaningful. Being kosher is about living with purpose, guided by values. In Jewish dietary law, this translates to divine directives, actions beyond mere convenience. In philanthropy, meaningful giving transcends just being generous. It aligns with deeper values and purposes, transforming giving into an expression of a person's ethos.

Mindful. Just as kosher eating involves careful consideration and awareness of what one consumes, mindful giving demands a thoughtful approach to philanthropy. It's not just about where or how much you give, but also includes understanding the broader impact of your contributions. This mindfulness extends to recognizing the needs of beneficiaries, the effectiveness of programs, and the long-term implications of your support. It also involves being consciously aware of the ripple effects your giving can generate, ensuring that your philanthropic efforts are not only well-intentioned, but also well-informed and responsible.

Measurable. Ultimately, kosher meaning and mindfulness drive action. Whether eating kosher food or conducting yourself in a kosher way, kosher is a practical and pragmatic expression of meaningful ideas and mindful planning. In the context of kosher giving, this means turning intentions and conscious actions into tangible results through direct aid, strategic partnerships, and/or innovative solutions. This aspect of kosher giving emphasizes seeing your values and goals materialize through effective philanthropic strategies and become real-world, measurable results.

Giving in Times of War

When discussing giving in times of war, the focus extends beyond merely responding to immediate needs. It's about understanding the complexities of a high-stakes environment where every contribution can have a significant impact.

War challenges us to reconsider our approach to giving. It demands speed, precision, and adaptability to ensure immediate and effective impact. This book explores how the dynamics of extreme situations influence philanthropic strategies, pushing us to act swiftly yet thoughtfully.

Our primary point of reference is the ongoing Hamas-Israel Iron Swords War. This war has led to a surge in needs, increased civilian engagement, and a wave of philanthropic generosity, creating both immense opportunities and significant challenges. We will explore strategies to match your resources more effectively with war-driven needs as well as how to align your well-intentioned efforts with meaningful outcomes.

Giving in Times of Peace

Peaceful times present various opportunities and challenges. These periods allow us to adopt a long-term perspective, plan strategically, and invest in the growth and maintenance of our communities.

In this book, we'll explore how giving in times of peace differs from crisis philanthropy. We'll examine the critical role of establishing strong foundations for future development, fostering lasting partnerships, and making a sustainable impact.

I invite you to join me in exploring how calm periods require a proactive, visionary approach to philanthropy, one that resonates with the enduring principles of kosher giving.

Keeping in mind both the intense scenarios of war and the stability of peace, we will explore:

- Potential opportunities and pitfalls in giving
- Effective methods for identifying needs
- Criteria for choosing the right partners in philanthropy
- Personal understanding of your giving purpose
- Steps to design, implement, evaluate, and refine your Kosher Giving Plan

How to Use This Book

This book offers a practical, step-by-step guide to enhancing your approach to philanthropy. Each chapter is built upon its predecessor, creating a comprehensive pathway to effective, kosher giving. You'll be equipped with tools and insights to assess needs, identify impactful projects, and measure your success. From understanding the foundational pillars of kosher giving to refining and adapting your strategies, this book serves as your personal guide to developing your own Kosher Giving Plan. Whether you're a seasoned philanthropist or just starting out, these pages will provide you with the means to make your giving more impactful and purposeful.

We'll begin by addressing the challenge of giving effectively and proceed to offer solutions. We'll discuss how to better align givers, recipients and the impact agents that help connect them. With these pillars of giving in mind. I'll lead you through the process of preparing your own, personal Kosher Giving Plan. We'll walk through the process step by step, ensuring you're equipped with the tools you need to adapt under changing, complex, or extreme circumstances.

Each chapter closes with "Kosher Food for Thought"—questions that encourage you to reflect, and "Kosher Giving Applied Actions" – practical steps to transform theory into action. In addition, we've prepared helpful resources to accompany your process of reflection and planning. Use our Kosher Giving Journal to chart your journey, and use our Kosher Giving Plan Workbook to clarify and quantify your path. These are free and available for you to download from our website at www.KosherGiving.com/tools.

Impact and Purpose

As described in this Preface, this book means a lot to me. It's my way of making sense of the chaos, my contribution to better giving, and a personal gift to a world that can use some fixing.

I don't expect this book to be as meaningful to you as it is to me. My modest hope is that you approach your giving with a fresh perspective and an openness to the best practices outlined below.

Ultimately, this book is about aligning our purpose with our impact. When I invite you to join me on this journey, I mean it. We're both contributing to and amplifying our impact. Knowing that we are collaborating on this path reassures me that we're headed in the right direction.

Now, Let's Get Started:

1. **Download the Kosher Giving Journal.** This will be your personal companion throughout our journey. It's designed for ease of use, helping you track your progress as

you consider our Kosher Food for Thought. The journal ensures that no insight is overlooked. Get your copy at www.KosherGiving.com/tools.

2. **Download the Kosher Giving Plan Workbook.** This spreadsheet-based workbook is your bridge from contemplation to action. It allows you to record everything from the scale of your efforts to their qualitative impact and transform what might have initially seemed like a mere collection of receipts into a carefully crafted plan. This plan, adaptable annually or seasonally, will help you reap the full benefits of this book, affecting both your growth and the lives touched by your future philanthropy. Download the template we created just for you at www.KosherGiving.com/tools

3. **Dedicate time.** Commit to more than just the time needed to read this book; invest in making the experience meaningful. Whether you prefer tea, coffee, or a glass of wine, create a conducive environment for reflection. Utilize the Journal and the Workbook at the end of each chapter. Remember, you might find it beneficial to revisit certain chapters or allocate more than one session to thoroughly absorb the content. Take your time, fully engage with the material, and embrace the deep sense of purpose that comes with your continuously developing impact.

Part 1: Principles for Better Giving

Chapter One

Crisis Giving Activated

Everything changed on October 7, 2023, both for Israel and for her global allies. Our perception of reality was turned upside down as a new, seemingly unforeseen war engulfed the country. The established norms of Israel's security were shattered, leaving too many pieces for a grieving nation to begin to collect. And, as the lines between the home front and the front lines blurred, a new reality began to emerge.

Hamas, known for the decades of terror it has waged against Israel, had long-ago turned rocket fire from the Gaza Strip at Israeli population centers into a regular, sometimes seasonal, occurrence. Their bombing, stabbing, and shooting attacks weren't new either. But this was the first time that it launched an all-out war on Israel, murdering over 1400 Israelis and kidnapping over 240 in the span of a single day.

Our focus is not on the Israeli Defense Force's initially slow but ultimately effective response to this declaration of war. Volumes will be written about the many misconceptions that left civilians and soldiers so painfully vulnerable to the onslaught. We're not going to delve into the Israeli government's reactions and responses or preoccupy ourselves with pointing a finger at who could have or should have done a better job, either. We're here to highlight and learn from the positive measures that were taken, considering the tragedy and despite its related challenges.

Israel is resilient. Israel's friends are committed. In times of crisis, our nation and its supporters are "all hands on deck," with everyone volunteering to do as much as they can. But is more always more? Do more needs plus more resources necessarily equal well aligned solutions?

The surge in giving has been impressive and inspirational. Israeli society's wholehearted commitment is a phenomenon to be studied, packaged, and shared across the globe. These are the aspects that were handled well during the war. That said, even what went right can be improved upon.

We'll start by exploring the opportunities that arose, then examine the challenges faced, and finally, navigate our way towards achieving a greater impact.

A Groundswell of Global Support

During the Iron Swords War, Jewish and Christian communities around the world mirrored their solidarity in past Israeli crises, significantly increasing their financial support to Israel and Israeli businesses and organizations. The contributions were diverse, focusing on helping those displaced by the war, strengthening non-profits capable of reaching the front lines, and, notably, efforts to protect Israel's reputation in the international court of public opinion and counter rising antisemitism.

The Jewish Federations of North America is one such example, which raised an extraordinary $638 million through its network of local Jewish communities. The UJA-Federation of New York, a major player in this network, allocated over $38 million for ground operations in Israel. And in a demonstration of support and confidence, Israel Bonds reported sales exceeding $200 million in bonds in the week following the Hamas attacks.. [1]

However, these remarkable figures also raise critical questions: Where does such a substantial amount of money go? How well do grass roots civil society initiatives align with the generous funds that were pledged and collected? And are both the efforts and the funds effectively aligned with the needs, at least in part?

It's widely acknowledged that the system isn't well designed for such extreme circumstances. But this realization carries with it a responsibility. When tending to needs and servicing philanthropists, we look to 'the system' to respond effectively.

In my conversations with donors, nonprofit leaders, and advisors, I noticed an interesting pattern emerging. During the first week of the crisis, generous donors sent significant sums to organizations that they were familiar with. Sometimes, they asked for details, but more often than not, they gave swiftly and unconditionally. In one case, I was told of a philanthropist who said there was no need to send a receipt. These givers understood the need to mobilize capital swiftly, and they sent those donations to their Israel-based partners without batting an eye.

But by week two, long before Israelis gave themselves permission to smile and as international opinion began to shift from unconditional support to increasing expressions of outright antisemitism, the pure enthusiasm of full-fledged support was tempered by a growing sense of pragmatism. People started asking more ques-

---

1. https://www.timesofisrael.com/us-jews-are-raising-money-for-an-israel-in-crisis-but-is-there-enough-to-go-around/

tions about how their donations were deployed, if any bottlenecks existed, and what they could expect going forward. The quality of the responses varied greatly from organization to organization.

Large, established organizations, while proficient in handling significant funds, sometimes found themselves in a holding pattern, safeguarding donations until they could develop appropriate allocation plans. Their strength lay in their ability to manage resources over the long term, but they struggled with immediate deployment of those resources due to the evolving nature of the crisis.

On the other hand, smaller, grassroots operations, more attuned to the immediate needs on the ground, faced difficulties either in securing the needed resources or in managing the financial reporting both short and long term. Their proximity to the crisis allowed them to identify and react to urgent needs quickly, but their inexperience in handling large funds impeded their ability to manage these resources effectively over time. As always, if 'heads' is an opportunity, then 'tails' is a challenge. When you care enough to give, you care enough to see to it that your gift is well stewarded-

.

There's a confidence that comes with experience, and there's a passion that comes with a clear sense of purpose. But when the two aren't sufficiently aligned, the donor is left wondering where to begin, who to work with and which causes to support.

Israel's Civil Society Steps Up

The global community's enthusiasm to give was matched, albeit not perfectly aligned, with a robust response from Israeli society. Israel saw an overnight surge in needs at individual, local, regional, and national levels, the likes of which can only be compared to a tsunami that wipes out entire communities, leaves every form of devastation in its path, and carries with it the threat of follow-up storms, at any given moment. In this case, however, the destruction was far more painful and unforgiving. It was brutal, intentional, unethical, and unimaginable. And it mobilized Israeli civil society like never before.

An academic study revealed that roughly half of all Israelis engaged in active volunteer work during the initial two weeks of the conflict. Because many reservists were called to duty, and the rest of the population held the fort down at home, just about everyone played a significant role. This massive effort was described as a "mega-event" for Israel's civil society, unparalleled in both scale and magnitude, as compared to past conflicts or crises, including the COVID pandemic.

Over 1,000 new civil initiatives were established in response to the war, addressing a wide variety of needs. These included support for soldiers, supplying equipment, aiding evacuated individuals, and providing psychological care for trauma victims. Interestingly, these efforts spanned across various segments of society, including Arab populations, highlighting a united front in times of national crisis.

About 28% of the volunteers were new to the world of volunteering, indicating a massive mobilization of previously unengaged individuals. The volunteer force was diverse and inclusive, spanning all age groups and nearly equal participation from men and women across religious and secular backgrounds. [2]

This social activism was also met by domestic philanthropy. An extraordinary wave of generosity washed over Israel, not just in a surge of volunteers but also in an unprecedented level of donations. Israelis, driven by a profound sense of solidarity, opened their hearts and wallets, supporting a broad spectrum of causes

---

2. https://www.timesofisrael.com/study-nearly-50-of-israeli-citizens-volunteered-during-first-weeks-of-war/

directly affected by the conflict. From aiding families who'd lost loved ones to providing essentials to soldiers at the front, the donations addressed grassroots needs across a closely-knit society where the war was widely felt.

This collective effort transcended typical divisions, uniting people across various backgrounds toward a shared purpose. It showcased Israeli society's resilience and capacity to rapidly mobilize in support of their community, setting a new benchmark for civic engagement and philanthropy during a national crisis.

Long before Israel's government had comprehensive plans for the home front, the growth of the non-profit sector was evident. The Registrar for Nonprofit Organizations began arranging how-to webinars to streamline the process of registering new organizations, and the Tax Authority made provisions to allow all non-profits to support the war effort without special permission, irrespective of their stated mandate.

As I write, we are six weeks into the war. There's a strong sense of purpose within the community. Whether you're wearing a non-profit's t-shirt or showing up at work to keep the economy going, civil society's engagement remains a central theme of the current war.

However, this spontaneous and wide-reaching mobilization has faced its share of challenges. The rapid organization of grassroots efforts often lacked coordination, resulting in duplicated tasks, logistical overlaps, and in some cases, unprepared volunteers dealing with traumatized survivors. Despite these issues, civil society significantly contributed to supporting Israel and its people, and a shared awareness emerged: a more efficient and organized approach could enhance our collective impact.

The 3 M's of Kosher Giving: Meaningful, Mindful, and Measurable

Roughly two weeks into the war, I was approached by a non-profit leader with a question about one of their leading donors. Inspired by his parents who had sold everything, including their dining room furniture, to support Israel during the 1967 Six-Day War, this donor saw the current war as his moment to follow in their footsteps. He was determined to donate the entirety of his family foundation's assets to aid Israel's efforts - as quickly as possible. This desire, driven by a powerful blend of personal history and present circumstances, underscored the deep emotional connection and sense of duty that motivated him to give in this time of crisis.

When asked for advice on managing this donor's intentions, and considering that a swift immediate contribution would likely be less impactful than a carefully planned approach to giving, I suggested a "yes-and" approach.

Sure, we should honor the donor's unyielding dedication, as it is rooted in a profound personal history, and a commitment to the cause. His enthusiasm, driven by emotion and the desire to act in an urgent crisis, is a testament to his deep-seated commitment to meaningful giving. And, if his funds are meant to be used "*for such a time as this*" (Book of Esther 4:14), then it's a worthy and commendable cause. But we can't stop there.

In addition to the "yes", there must be an "and." Philanthropy requires more than meaningful commitment alone. It demands a mindful approach to resource allocation. Mindful giving is characterized by strategic thinking, where decisions on donations are driven by a clear understanding of the impact - the needs on the ground and the long-term implications of the aid provided. Mindful philanthropy also involves asking hard questions: How will this money be used? What are the most pressing needs? Who are the best partners to ensure the funds are utilized effectively?

Then there's the other 'and,' one that's no less significant than meaningful and mindful giving. It's the need for our giving to be measurable, to generate outcomes, and positive impact.

Ensuring that a donor's hard-earned resources are used philanthropically demands the same level of care and effectiveness as one would apply to a capital investment. What starts with a commitment to meaningful giving should evolve into mindful planning and tangible outcomes.

Meaningful, mindful, and measurable are the three core kosher principles guiding our giving. This donor, with good intentions, considers liquidating his family foundation for the war, a meaningful gesture. Yet, the mindfulness of his giving warrants consideration. His motivation is clear, but does he fully consider the specific applications of his donations beyond general war relief efforts? As he plans to liquidate, engaging in a mindful approach, questions arise. If obstacles prevent immediate use of the funds, will he maintain his giving pace, or wait until his contributions can be effectively managed and utilized?

A Lesson in Better Giving

The first lesson in kosher giving is that we can always give better. It's the recognition that, while the act of giving is inherently positive, there is always room to enhance our giving with better quality and better impact. This means taking a more thoughtful approach to where and how we allocate our resources, ensuring that our giving is not just generous but also effective, targeted, and aligned with real needs. It involves educating ourselves about the causes we support, understanding the complexities involved, and collaborating with organizations that can use our donations effectively.

This, to maximize the positive impact of our donations, turning generosity into significant change.

Kosher giving means asking thoughtful questions, so that what we contribute to the world around us is marked by quality and value. It means thinking before you give, not to slow your impact but to increase it.

In the next chapter, we'll begin to identify the three pillars of kosher giving, each rooted in the kosher concepts of meaningful, mindful, and measurable philanthropy. But before diving into the details of giving and building our own giving plans, there is an additional insight that our liquidating philanthropist invites us to explore, one we may never bother asking ourselves: why do we give?

The Hebrew term for charity is *tzedakah*, translated as righteousness. From the very first scriptural mention of *tzedakah* in the context of charitable giving, an extensive list of reasons is provided to explain 'why' giving is so consequential. It's a passage in the Book of Genesis that speaks to the timeless nature of giving, as well as to the uncompromising values that drive us to act on behalf of others.

> "And the Lord said, "Shall I conceal from Abraham what I am doing? And Abraham will become a great and powerful nation, and all the nations of the world will be blessed in him. For I have known him because he directs his sons and his household after him, that they should keep the way of the Lord to perform righteousness and justice, in order that the Lord bring upon Abraham that which He spoke concerning him." ***Genesis 18: 17-19***

G-d[3] is about to destroy the cities of Sodom and Gomorrah, but not before he invites Abraham to discuss his plans. G-d provides several reasons for speaking to on this matter. One reason is that He wants Abraham to instruct his family in ethical behavior, which will then shape the morals of an entire nation, ultimately benefiting the whole world. However, beyond these future virtues and impacts, a more basic reason for God's decision to involve Abraham is evident.

"For I have known him." The fundamental reason why G-d chooses to inform Abraham of the plans to destroy these cities is that G-d knows Abraham. He knows that Abraham will not allow this to happen without a confrontation. He knows that Abraham will challenge Him. He knows that Abraham will argue that the virtue of *tzedakah* has the power to bend or overcome the virtue of justice. G-d knows Abraham's DNA. He knows not only that Abraham is a giver, but that Abraham personifies the quality of giving.

We can list reasons for giving, and we can explain how giving provides benefit in the short and long term, but the logical explanations are preceded by the deeper meaning and values at the heart of giving. Kosher giving is a personality trait, a personal quality that defines us. We don't ask why we give the same way that we don't ask why we're happy, why we're entrepreneurial or why we're compassionate. We give because that's who we are.

The distinction between core values, logical explanations and ultimate outcomes is instructive. Our family foundation friend wants to give because he is a committed and motivated giver. It's just how

---

3. According to the practice of Torah Judaism, it is customary to spell 'G-d' with a hyphen out of respect for the sanctity of the name.

he's wired. He doesn't want to miss an opportunity to give where it counts. But is caring enough?

The lesson learned from Abraham is that not all forms of tzedakah lead to the desired impact at the desired time. Abraham indeed challenged his Creator, advocating for the doomed cities. His persuasive efforts led G-d to consider sparing them if righteous individuals were found. However, no such people were found. Abraham's noble intentions, rooted in the value of tzedakah, did not yield the happy ending that he was hoping for: "And Abraham returned to his place." (Genesis 18:33)

Abraham's desire to give wasn't misguided. He was invited into the dialogue not to fail but to learn a painful and compelling lesson. Yes, we need to jump at the opportunity to give. And yes, we need to enlist our minds and dedicated effort to influence reality thoughtfully. But even then, it's important to remember that the act of giving, caring, and going beyond ourselves, does not always translate into impact.

In crisis situations, whether in Abraham's time or in war today, we must seek and seize opportunities to give better. Giving better means committing ourselves to the full range of kosher principles, giving in a way that is meaningful, mindful, and measurable.

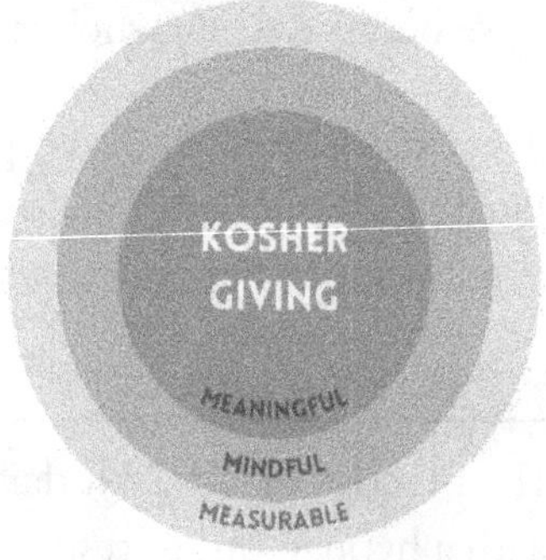

The Core of Kosher Giving

The meaning of giving is at the core, the starting point that motivates us to act. From there, we move outward to a mindful approach, discerning opportunities, identifying worthy partners, and navigating challenges. Yet, our efforts are incomplete without seeing tangible, measurable results. We want to see impact in that third outer circle. Whether change happens rapidly or unfolds over generations, our focus encompasses the entire journey, from initial intentions to ultimate outcomes.

Kosher Food for Thought

What does meaningful giving mean to you? Why do you give? How does philanthropy reflect who you are as a person?

What does mindful giving mean to you? In what ways do your current giving practices reflect a thoughtful, strategic approach? Where might there be room for improvement?

How do you drive your giving towards measurable impact? How do you balance your personal motivations for giving with the practical considerations of effective philanthropy?

Kosher Giving Applied Actions

1. Download the Kosher Giving Journal from https://www.KosherGiving.com/tools.

2. Use the journal to track your responses to the Kosher Food for Thought above and dedicate time to your renewed philanthropic journey. This will serve as a basis for your Kosher Giving Plan.

3. In the spaces provided, use the journal to describe your meaningful, mindful, and measurable giving in the past, and compare your descriptions with your goals for the future.

Chapter Two

Crisis Giving Pitfalls

Cracks and Gaps

Across the giving terrain, as with any social landscape with multiple partners, there are inherent fissures - subtle cracks that are, under everyday circumstances, manageable, if not entirely unnoticeable. These fissures, which represent some of the challenges in philanthropy, could include cracks created by misaligned expectations between donors and beneficiaries, communication gaps, and logistical inefficiencies. However, during a crisis like the Iron Swords War, these fissures can rapidly widen into chasms. The sudden surge in needs, coupled with a flood of resources and new operators, amplifies these existing challenges. The overwhelming influx of aid, although well-intentioned, might not always sync with the real needs on the ground - or the capacity to effectively manage it, sometimes leading to counterproductive outcomes.

***

My friend Mike Humphrey, a seasoned philanthropist and a volunteer non-profit lay leader, once shared his perspective during our social impact work. Occasionally, we had more resources than we expected for a given need. Mike would smile and say, “well, we have a ‘high-class problem’ on our hands.” “It’s like we say in Israel, Mike”, I would respond. “These are ‘rich man’s problems’”.

On a small scale, high-class problems are not only tolerable — they’re desirable. Extra funding for a program can potentially enhance a project’s outcomes or enable future sustainable engagement. It can also mean that there are more contributors to a project than expected, expanding the network for future collaborations.

However, when such excess becomes systemic, turning into an overload across multiple projects, it can turn pre-existing cracks in the system into gaping holes.

The giving chain includes a series of exchanges, each with potential cracks where inefficiencies can take hold. In the previous chapter, we focused on a sincere, at times infectious, drive to give. This led us to address the basic kosher principles of meaningful, mindful, and measurable giving. But how can we quantify these principles? What does meaningful giving feel like? How can we map out the process of mindful giving? And when we want to track our impact, how can measurable giving be measurable?

Our 3 M’s of meaningful, mindful and measurable are relevant for all types of kosher. As we apply these principles to giving, we define them in concrete pragmatic terms. If these principles are at the base of our philanthropy, then we need to apply them in such a way that they will serve as supports for our Kosher Giving Plan. This requires us to speak not only in terms of kosher giving principles, but in terms of the 3 pillars of kosher giving as well.

Meaningful giving is best expressed as a person's or organization’s purpose. Mindful giving is relevant throughout the giving process, but when expressed as a pillar, it’s primarily focused on the work done by and with our impact agents. And measurable giving, also relevant throughout the process, is most focused on causes and impact, defined as the needs pillar of our emerging structure.

Pillars of Kosher Giving

Let's begin with purpose. The gentleman who wanted to liquidate his family foundation to support war relief projects was stalled at the stage of life purpose. Purpose is related but not identical to meaningful giving. This individual's heartfelt commitment lacked nothing by way of meaning. It was all heart, marked by enough dedication to fuel his personal drive to make a significant contribution. However, it lacked a defined purpose. Purpose goes beyond meaning; it is inherently directional. Being purposeful means working towards a specific goal, a goal that transcends personal motivation and reaches towards thoughtful impact.

We'll have an opportunity to dive into our giving purpose in the chapters ahead. For now, let's keep in mind that we should think twice before pointing fingers at others when good philanthropic intentions go sideways. Sometimes, the issue is not our partners but our own intense focus on meaning, which may not always translate into a broader, well-defined goal-oriented purpose. Meaning is focused on what giving means to us, while purpose directs us to think through how that giving will affect others. In times of crisis, this distinction is even more critical than under normative circumstances.

Holes in the Armor

Were you approached with a request to fund bulletproof vests? Did you contribute? Did the vests make it to their destination?

As Israel's reservists flowed towards the war front *en masse*, the Ministry of Defense faced unexpected challenges. First, the draft was met with well over 100% participation, fed by the same spirit of community volunteerism that mobilized the home front. Tens of thousands of uninvited reservists were warmly welcomed, but the system struggled to adequately support them all. Another challenge, characteristic of a war in 2023, was the easy access to cell phones and extensive personal contact lists. If global connectivity is measured in six degrees of separation, then an Israeli reservist group is just a WhatsApp message away from a wide array of contacts.

Israelis often follow their Defense Forces' orders with respect and sincerity, yet they frequently question the reliability of 'the system.' When the new enlistees showed up for battle only to discover that they were lacking life-saving gear, they took to their cell phones, leveraging connections and technology to raise funds and procure bulletproof vests and other tactical gear.

It took some time, but eventually, the Ministry of Defense agreed to allow soldiers to use non-standard gear. However, the contributed gear still needed to go through a licensing process, ensuring that it met IDF combat standards. Bulletproof vests that failed to offer proper protection were rejected, and those not suitably camouflaged had to be returned.

Yael Eckstein, President and CEO of the International Fellowship of Christians and Jews (IFCJ), explained in a KosherGiving.com video interview how her organization steered away from these challenges. IFCJ is the largest non-profit in Israel, with an extensive network of relationships in government and civil society. Their commitment to supporting Israel's security is one of their three core domains of experience and expertise, along with tending to the poor and encouraging *aliyah* (immigration) to Israel. With their deep understanding of the urgent needs, and their appreciation of the complexities involved in addressing those needs effectively, identifying precisely where they could be most helpful proved to be the best policy.

As Yael explained, IFCJ prides itself on effective giving. They develop clear giving criteria and execute according to plan. This has been the case since the founding of the organization. "My father, Rabbi Yechiel Eckstein of blessed memory, wanted to make sure that we give in the best way possible," she said.

It's no wonder that one of their donors approached Yael with a 1.5-million-dollar blank check at the start of the war. "I know how you work, Yael. I respect your giving ethic and professionalism. I know these funds are in good hands with the Fellowship," the donor stated.

For the Fellowship, understanding the challenges of contributing directly to the IDF while staying true to their commitment to Israel's security on the other meant charting an innovative path forward. They did not send shipments of tactical gear directly to the Ministry of Defense, nor did they follow individual requests for support down unpredictable rabbit holes. Instead, ICFJ leveraged their extensive network of municipalities to address the acute need for upgrading security, a need felt on the home front and experienced most directly by ill-equipped first responder teams. Within the first weeks of the war, the Fellowship contributed 5,000 protective vests to the members of local security forces across Israeli border communities. These communities' needs were pressing following the October 7 attacks, amid fear of having to defend themselves, should similar infiltrations occur in the future.

But IFCJ was the exception to the rule. It's not easy to purchase bulletproof vests by the thousands. And even if you could, who's to say that your generous gift will reach your intended destination? Even if it was your neighbor's cousin, or your cousin for that matter, who set the request for support in motion, that doesn't mean that by the time the vests clear customs and are processed by the Ministry of Defense, that they will necessarily reach his or her unit and that they will personally benefit from the thoughtful and generous gift. When donor intentions, the process of giving and the ability to address needs are misaligned, then outcomes and impact are unlikely to meet expectations.

***

Impact Agents

Bridging the gap between donors and beneficiaries involves numerous players, including people, organizations, and institutions that develop programs and solutions. These bridge-builders, or **impact agents** as we will refer to them, are crucial in turning purpose into impact, have good intentions, but executing these intentions effectively is easier said than done.

Our impact agents are the essential links that connect givers' intentions to beneficiaries in need, transforming philanthropic purpose into tangible, real-world impact. They're program operators, non-profit organizations, intermediaries, and institutions. Each plays a critical part in ensuring that any donated resources are utilized effectively and reach those in need. In the context of bridging philanthropic intent with actual needs, mindful giving involves a thoughtful, informed approach to selecting and working with these impact agents, ensuring alignment with our goals and values and of the ability to execute our vision well.

During crises like the Iron Swords War, philanthropists often respond with swift generosity, not fully considering the logistical and regulatory challenges, such as IDF gear standards and soldiers' deployment needs. This gap between donor intentions and actual needs highlights the central role of impact agents.

> **Quick actions, driven more by speed than precision, can lead to misalignments, overwhelming the capacity for effective resource distribution and utilization.**

As crisis situations rapidly evolve, what may initially seem like an effective contribution can quickly become obsolete. There are simply countless pitfalls that impact agents need to address, avoid, and resolve.

As individuals, organizations, and funders work to recoup funds that were caught up in large-scale contributions that never reached their intended recipients, a reactionary recoil sometimes sets in. If you or someone you know was dissatisfied with the outcome of a donation, you might think twice before giving again. This is where gaps across the philanthropy chain can have broader implications, challenging not only the impact agents but also the very causes in need of support.

What Do You Need?

The community of Eliav was established in 2004 and is situated between Be'er Sheva and Kiryat Gat. Eliav is home to 200 religious and secular families with a diverse array of opinions, professions, and backgrounds.

Located 30 kilometers from Gaza on one side, and just 300 meters from the security fence with Judea and Samaria (commonly known as the West Bank) on the other, Eliav lies in close proximity to two Arab villages that are known for supporting Hamas and aiding terrorists. While the security standards in Eliav were thought to be adequate, the events of October 7th demonstrated just how exposed and vulnerable the community really is.

With no permanent IDF presence in Eliav and the nearest police station 30 minutes away, Eliav's team of volunteer first responders, only modestly equipped, are the primary line of defense against potential infiltrations during this period of increased terrorist threats. Yet, at the start of the war, these first responders faced a lack of basic equipment for self-defense and protecting residents. Fortunately, Dr. Ilana Kwartin, an Eliav resident and mother of four, had their safety in mind. An influential figure in Women's Rights, the author of "Imprisoned: Women in Extreme Controlling Relationships", holder of a PhD, and founder and CEO of Levana.ai, a woman-focused precision medicine platform, Dr. Ilana Kwartin juggles various significant roles. When not managing her children's carpool, Ilana is actively working to make the world a better place.

Confronted with challenges, Ilana identifies opportunities. She launched an online campaign to raise funds for local security needs. As she sees it, this was not a request for handouts, but for partnership. "I've absorbed Zionism from my mother's milk, through our *aliyah* to Israel before the fall of the Iron Curtain, in my days as an emissary of Israel to the United States and in recent years through the growth of the Eliav community," she explained. "Living in this region isn't easy, but we are undeterred. We just need the means to be able to defend ourselves."

They got off to a strong start, but roughly halfway through their 300,000 USD campaign, they stalled, as initial enthusiasm was met with skepticism. "People were asking tough questions,", Ilana recalled. "'How can you say the Israeli government doesn't provide the necessary equipment?' or 'Who says you need any of this equipment at all?'" These queries reflect the complex dynamics of donor confidence and beneficiary accountability.

Ilana quickly identified the cracks that were becoming pitfalls.

It was more than just unfulfilled promises of bulletproof vests. Ilana pointed out several issues: "First, there was misinformation, with rumors that Hamas was deceptively fundraising under the guise of Israeli nonprofits. Second, Eliav's obscurity—it's a small community unknown to most Israelis and foreigners. And what about those unfamiliar with the IsraelGives platform hosting our campaign?" She realized donors were questioning the legitimacy of both her role as a impact agent and of Eliav as a beneficiary.

But questioning the needs, as Ilana explained, ran deeper than the extreme circumstances at hand. It highlighted a pre-war disconnect between donors and beneficiaries, a gap that the war began to challenge. "I remember volunteering in the Ukraine at the beginning of the war with Russia. Generous donors from America, some who I knew from my time as an Israeli emissary in Los Angeles, would send over suitcases of dry goods that they purchased from Target. It wasn't what the Ukrainian recipients needed, and it wasn't the most efficient form of support. I made it my business to communicate to the donors how their gifts were making an impact, and how the needs could be better met."

Ilana's experiences in Ukraine shaped her approach in Eliav. She personally addressed each inquiry, providing transparency and reassurance about her authenticity and the community's urgent needs, followed by regular updates. "People donated, and then donated again, asking what more they could do. Our campaign became IsraelGives' most successful private initiative."

Both Yael Eckstein of IFCJ and Dr. Ilana Kwartin of the Eliav community successfully grappled with some of the potential pitfalls linked to crisis giving. Yael teaches us that professional and adept organizations can mindfully identify red flags and help prevent impact pitfalls. Similarly, Ilana's efforts demonstrate the impact of clear communication with donors, so that their contributions manifest themselves as measurable results.

Their experiences and effectiveness encourage us to see past potential pitfalls in philanthropy. Effective philanthropy is rooted in our meaningful, mindful, and measurable giving. In turn, these three kosher principles become the foundation for our Kosher Giving Plan when applied as the practical pillars that can be quantified, tracked and refined: purpose, impact agents and needs. After defining the principle of meaningful giving in terms of direction and goal-oriented purpose, Yael and Ilana's experiences invite us to define measurable outcomes in terms of the needs and causes that we support, and mindful philanthropy in terms of the impact agents who operate programs and handle the flow of resources. Each of these pillars is necessary, and most effective when synchronized each with the other.

The 3 Pillars of Kosher Giving

There's a traditional Jewish worldview that helps us appreciate the need for not one pillar, but three.

The second teaching in the tractate of Pirkei Avot[1] (lit. Chapters of Fathers) states:

> *"On three things the world stands: on the Torah, on the service and on acts of lovingkindness".*

If society stands on a three-legged pedestal, then none of the legs can be compromised. The world requires a combination of knowledge, the application of that scholarship through service, and the fulfillment of needs through lovingkindness to persist. If one of these three pillars is missing, then the other two cannot continue to carry humanity forward.

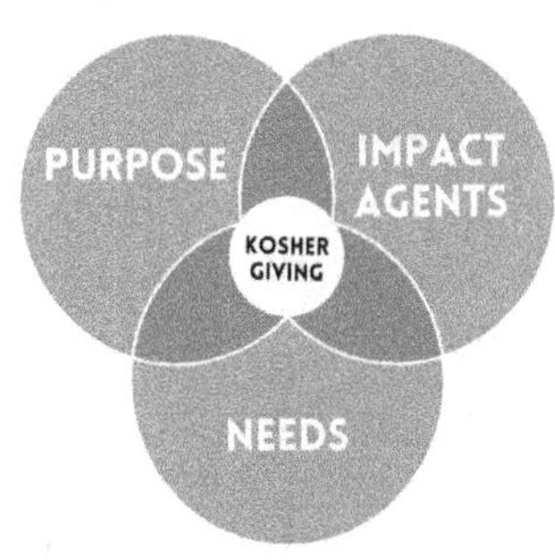

3 Pillars of Kosher Giving

While not identical, this teaching aligns with the ideas of meaningful, mindful, and measurable giving. It addresses the 'why' behind purpose, the 'how' of working with impact agents, and the 'what' of fulfilling needs across the spectrum of kosher giving.

Each of these pillars is necessary, and each needs the others to continue to be relevant and impactful. Understanding the interconnectedness of the three pillars is essential to creating your Kosher Giving Plan. These pillars collectively inform the strategy, execution, and impact of your philanthropic efforts. As we will discover in the

---

1. The Mishna is the first written codification of the Oral Torah, organized between the second and third centuries. Pirkei Avot is a tractate within the Nezikin order of the Mishna.

upcoming chapters, our grasp of these pillars paves the path to well-aligned and effective giving.

The Goal: Well Aligned Giving

Before we proceed, let's take a closer look at our pedestal. Note that it's not tilted or falling over. Our pedestal was designed not by an inexperienced hobbyist but by a careful and precise carpenter, who thoughtfully calculates the length of each leg before affixing the platform on top. He understands that it's not enough to have 3 pillars, but that they need to be well aligned to provide effective support.

Meaningful, mindful, and measurable are the kosher principles that guide us. Purpose, impact agents and needs are our pillars, the real-world expressions of those principles as they relate to our giving. When our pillars are aligned, they can substantiate untold opportunities for good, growth, development, and lasting impact. But if we neglect to align our pillars, or overlook one or more of them altogether, then we cannot expect our giving to realize its potential.

So, let's take the time to take a closer look. Let's examine our kosher giving pillars to better appreciate what we're looking for, and to better plan for meaningful impact. In the coming chapters, we'll explore each of the pillars, each of which will become a central theme of our Kosher Giving Plan.

Kosher Food for Thought

What is your giving purpose? Reflect on a recent philanthropic contribution you made. Did it align with your deeper purpose for giving? How did this contribution reflect your values and intentions?

Who are your impact agents? Think about an impact agent you've worked with. Were they effective in understanding and implementing your vision? How could mindfulness improve your selection and collaboration with impact agents in the future?

How do you identify needs? Recall a situation where your donation was intended to address a specific need. Did it generate the outcome you expected? What lessons did you learn about aligning your contributions more closely with the beneficiaries' actual needs?

Kosher Giving Applied Actions

1. **Track your giving chain.** Using your Kosher Giving Journal, which can be downloaded at koshergiving.com/tools. To do so, identify a contribution that was meaningful to you and indicate which parties were involved in processing the funds and translating them into action in the space provided.

2. **Along your giving chain, use the checklist provided to identify gaps.** Are all the steps in the giving process accounted for? Do you have all the necessary information or are you unaware, either of the work process or of the outcomes and impact?

3. **Identify opportunities for improvement.** Have you and your impact agents successfully grappled with chal-

lenges? Have you been able to avoid pitfalls? Articulate goals for an improved giving chain.

Chapter Three

Pillar 1 - Know the Needs

I said a silent prayer before speaking with Vered Adar, but that didn't stop the tears from flowing.

Vered is a survivor. She and her daughter managed to escape the terrorist onslaught of the Nir Oz Kibbutz. Sadly, many of their loved ones did not.

We spoke on the fifth day of the war. Only a week earlier, Nir Oz had been a community of 350 resilient residents, accustomed—if it can be described that way—to rocket fire from nearby Gaza. As of our October 12 interview, they had estimated that 70 community-members were unaccounted for and that 30 were confirmed dead, but it was too chaotic to know for sure.

Vered spoke to me from a hotel in Eilat, normally considered a vacation spot in better times. The hellish experience of hearing stories from other survivors, about 170 of which were staying at the same hotel, was tempered by the comfort of knowing that the remnants of the community were sticking together.

Like so many frontline Israeli civilians, Vered is strong. But there were places in our conversation that we agreed not to delve into. As Vered led the conversation, she shared that Yaffa Adar, one of the iconic illustrations of this war, is her mother.

Yaffa is an 85-year-old Hamas captive. She was driven off in a golf cart, and as of this writing, no one has heard from her since. (Fortunately, before this book went to print, Yaffa was released and returned to her family.)

Vered's nieces, Yaffa's granddaughters, were interviewed across the globe. There's a story that needs to be told, but it's challenging to get the message across when there were two significant unknowns: what happened, and where they go from here.

When I asked Vered about their online fundraising campaign and what they're raising money for, she responded with an honest, straightforward answer: "We will see."

"I don't have a home to return to," Vered explained, "and I don't know if I can bring myself to return. When we can organize ourselves, we will sit down with the kibbutz Chief Financial Officer and community leadership. Then, we will see."

In normal circumstances, organizations can and should be expected to define the parameters of the programs and outcomes that will be affected by the generous donations of funders. But there are exceptions to the rule, when we focus exclusively on the partners we work with even before we know what they plan to do with the funding. Kibbutz Nir-Oz at the outset of the war is one such exception.

Considering the extent of the chaos and carnage, there is simply no alternative for Kibbutz Nir Oz. They need to build reserves so that they are prepared for when it's time to rebuild. But if the kibbutz, for obvious reasons, can't clearly characterize what they're raising funds for, how can donors be expected to know how to identify needs?

Just to be clear, this is not only a question for the individual donor, who may not have a staff at his disposal to do homework and research giving opportunities. Both in normal times and in times of war, foundations, funds, and non-profit organizations are all faced with the same question: What are the needs?

Wartime Needs Assessment Tools

Assessing needs can be approached in various ways. For those not facing situations as dire as Vered Adar's, who is grappling with the aftermath of her neighbors' murder and her mother's abduction, it's important to select a method for deciding what to support. In both war and peace, the question arises: where do we start?

Whereas some have no recourse but to adopt a gradual pace to assessing needs, others have taken the opposite approach, undertaking to make sense of the full range of needs in a relatively short period of time. Several private and public initiatives surfaced during the Iron Swords War. These organizations were established to assess needs and make information accessible to those who wanted to educate themselves on the situation as it unfolds.

One of the hallmarks of this war, when compared with other conflicts in the previous century, is the access to online information through news sites, social media and platforms that are dedicated to current events. This information availability means engagement can take many forms, depending on how it's organized.

For instance, the Mosaic United website, an initiative of the Israel Ministry of Diaspora Affairs, introduced a new interface. This Ministry, a governmental entity, is committed to strengthening ties between Israel and Jewish communities worldwide, promoting

Jewish identity and heritage. During crises like the ongoing conflict in Israel, the Ministry plays a crucial role in mobilizing support and coordinating relief efforts both in Israel and within the global Jewish community.

Through its Mosaic United Israel Aid Network, the Ministry of Diaspora Affairs has created a platform that connects donors, organizations, and individuals impacted by the conflict. This strategic platform is a means of assessing needs and aligning them with resources.

This approach addresses the question of where to begin. Projects are categorized according to themes such as education, elderly support, disabilities, food supply, advocacy, housing, volunteer support, and medical care. Donors can visit the site, search by topic, and discover lists of potential beneficiaries. If you have a clear idea of what you're looking for, you're likely to find a fitting option.

Another online Israeli government initiative is the Israel Rises platform. More than a website, Israel Rises is an ambitious collaboration of municipalities, non-governmental organizations, and businesses to match needs with resources. The site showcases 259 municipalities, 654,000 volunteers, 600,000 businesses, 1,000 companies and investors, 90 local foundations, 23 government - offices, 5 desk heads, and 600 funders from around the world. The numbers are indeed impressive.

Israel Rises also prioritizes national-scale needs, provides constant updates, and oversees end-to-end grant requests. As with Mosaic United, potential beneficiaries can submit requests for support, but Israel Rises goes further, using an internal evaluation to select which projects to display.

However, when it comes to these platforms, we have no way of knowing how they vet the causes. What are their criteria? How do they determine which projects qualify for aid? And, in the case of

Israel Rises, how do they prioritize select projects from a dizzying array of opportunities?

The third tool, while less ambitious than the previous two, has a more donor-centric focus.

Two days into the war, our team at Sector4 Strategy wondered how we could be of impact, despite not being on the front. Sector4 is an Israel-based advisory, committed to the success of the three sectors of the economy, government, business, and nonprofit, and to the development of the fourth sector, where the first three sectors converge and synergize. We knew that our experience working with both funders and beneficiaries could be a force multiplier, but how could we offer that experience beyond the specific clients we were already serving?

We also decided to leverage technology. Without the resources of the Israeli government at our disposal, we took a more modest approach. We started sourcing causes across our networks to bring the donor community direct access to projects that could potentially be of interest to them.

We did not do a comprehensive analysis of Israel's 40,000 nonprofit organizations. At no point did we try to develop a top-down hierarchy of priorities. And we are transparent about the fact that we do not conduct a thorough audit of each project as it surfaces. Instead, we describe the results of our vetting process, provide accurate information about each giving opportunity, and stress that the donor should be the one to decide which causes to support.

And so, the platform was launched two weeks into the war. The site offers daily updates about causes and insightful tools for donors. Advantageous as it is for the organizations that are featured on the site, we measure success not in terms of donations, but in terms of the growth of the donor community and the subscriptions to the KosherGiving.com newsletter.

Every featured cause opens with a story, followed by a description of the project on offer and a link to a third-party site for giving. We're not in the business of processing donations, but instead, focus wholeheartedly on providing donors with information. Our motto, "informed giving is better giving", sums our approach up well.

The most important parts of each feature are the "Kosher Status" and "Fine Print" sections. The Kosher Status delves into the principles of mindful and measurable giving. Here, we clearly address what we know about the organization's track record, governance, and transparency, providing benchmarks for potential donors. However, the importance of this section is fully realized only when coupled with our concluding section.

Each feature closes with the "Fine Print" (which appears in large letters) section. It reads:

Kosher Giving is dedicated to providing information and insights about charitable projects to assist donors in making informed decisions. While we strive to offer valuable resources and vetted information, we do not endorse or recommend specific projects. Ultimately, the choice to support a particular project is a personal decision that should align with your individual philanthropic goals and values.

We've considered implementing scoring systems or rankings for projects and nonprofits. However, our Editorial Board chose not to make this a priority. Instead, we've published our 'Kosher Criteria' on the site, providing a transparent guide for the giving community. This approach also acknowledges that determining needs is a judgement call. Whether it's our team sourcing and vetting the opportunities that appear on the site, walking you through the process of giving with personally tailored consulting services, or you're the one doing the research from start to finish about which causes to support, mindful giving is about learning, discerning, and making decisions.

Methodologies

Methodologies in philanthropy vary, and regardless of whether you're working with a team, a trusted partner, or independently, it's important to choose an effective approach for assessing needs. Each approach adds its distinct value, shaping the way you understand and respond to the needs around you.

The following is a shortlist of approaches to consider when assessing causes and needs:

Let's start off with the **community engagement and collaboration** approach. Engaging directly with those affected offers invaluable insights into their real needs, concerns, and the challenges they face. Collaborating with local organizations, which have an intimate understanding of each community's dynamics, can significantly enhance the effectiveness of your philanthropic efforts. This approach ensures that your support is relevant and responsive to the actual needs on the ground, as building strong connections with community members and local entities is key to a meaningful and impactful needs assessment.

Next is a **data-based approach**. This involves gathering quantifiable information through surveys, interviews, and research. Data helps gain a clearer, objective understanding of the needs, while consulting experts provide deeper insights. This approach ensures that your philanthropic actions are informed by solid evidence, targeting resources more effectively.

Accessing reliable data and expert advice can be challenging, especially in rapidly changing or crisis-driven situations. In the situation described above, when different government agencies, both with extensive networks, present different types of expert-cultivated needs listings, it's not easy to determine who to turn to. To address these challenges, you can use technology and networks to your advantage. Online surveys and data collection can be used to study trends and needs or to encourage beneficiaries to submit requests for support. Network development can also serve you well, should you have the time and resources to cultivate contacts who can provide timely insights or direct you to relevant data. These are difficult measures to undertake on your own. In the coming chapters, we'll discuss how professional partners, such as Sector4, can support you.

The third approach involves **ongoing assessment and adaptability**, emphasizing the importance of continuously updating and adjusting philanthropic strategies in response to changing circumstances. This method involves setting up regular feedback mechanisms with project beneficiaries and staying up to date on relevant developments. Additionally, planning for flexibility in philanthropic initiatives allows for necessary adjustments and ensures that responses remain on point. By developing responsive systems that can quickly adapt to new information or changing conditions, this approach assures you that your philanthropy is not only responsive but continues to make a meaningful and lasting impact.

This approach is not just for foundations or large organizations; it can be effectively tailored to individual donors as well. Even as a solo philanthropist, you can set up simple yet effective feedback mechanisms, such as direct conversations with beneficiaries or regular updates from project leaders. Additionally, combining this approach with others like community engagement and data-driven strategies can ensure a well-rounded and responsive philanthropic approach that adapts to changing needs and complements overall giving strategies.

The fourth approach is one of **comprehensive understanding**. This method balances empathy with practicality, understanding both immediate and long-term community needs for sustainable impact. It involves considering cultural sensitivities and encouraging community participation, ensuring a holistic view of your philanthropic efforts.

Whereas it's premature for Vered Adar to determine Nir Oz's specific needs, she immediately refers us to the fact that there's a system of accountability that is run by the kibbutz secretariat. Even without a bottom line, we're given a baseline of transparency. Mosaic United is different. We know about many causes, but we don't know about their vetting process. Israel Rises is, in some ways, more enigmatic. On one hand, we are reassured about the integrity of their operation as Israel's Homefront Command decides which projects to prioritize. But while we may accept the Israel Defense Forces' actions at face value during wartime without demanding extra transparency, the selection of only a few programs from the site's hundreds of thousands of affiliates naturally piques visitors' curiosity.

Before you choose which causes to support, it's best to know which of the causes' needs are current. This is true under normative circumstances, and although it's more challenging in times of war or crisis, it's even more important.

The methods listed above are points of departure, but they're not scientific formulas. Each represents an element of due diligence, inviting you to consider which factors are most important to you and how to begin your search for the projects that might fit your giving plan.

The What of Giving

If our kosher principles are our theoretical framework for giving, then we need to erect our Kosher Giving Plan upon a stable, practical foundation that can be clearly defined. We initiated our study of kosher principles with meaningful giving at the core, followed by mindful giving and closing with measurable giving. We started with what drives us, moving outwards towards impact. But when we lay the foundation for our Kosher Giving Plan by erecting the pragmatic pillars of our pedestal, we have more flexibility. Sometimes we begin with our purpose, other times with needs, and then there are situations where the giving plan begins with a commitment to an impact agent or an organization. The dynamics of pragmatism require us to take all three pillars into account, to align them with one another, and to recognize that there is no one single catalyst for kosher giving.

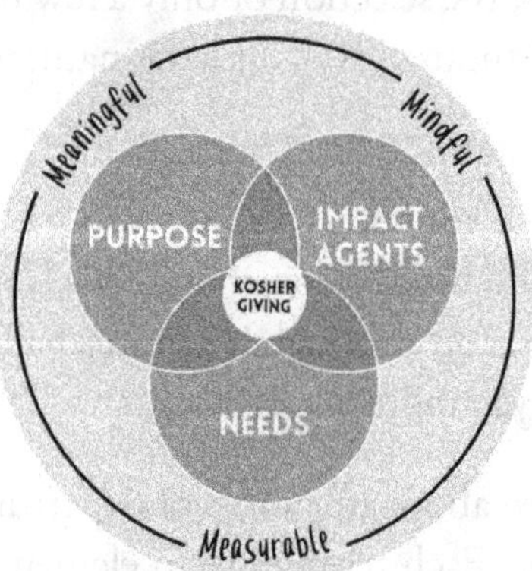

The Kosher Giving Framework

This might seem counterintuitive. After all, if we want to give meaningfully and mindfully, then maybe we should insist on identifying our purpose in giving before we try to process and prioritize the needs. Indeed, we don't want our giving to be a matter of convenience or circumstance alone, but there is a strong case to be made for exploring our philanthropy through the lens of the beneficiary.

One of the harsh realities of life is that there are always needs to fill. There's a sobering verse that puts things in perspective.

> For there will never cease to be needy ones in your land, which is why I command you: open your hand to the poor and needy kin in your land.
> **Deuteronomy 15:11**

At a glance, the notion that "there will never cease to be needy ones in your land" might seem disheartening. It raises questions about our efforts to combat poverty, address educational disparities, tackle inequality, and rebuild communities after conflict and violence. This perspective might appear to be a dampener on our aspirations for a better world.

Yet, the presence of needs is an undeniable reality. While no single person or organization can meet all the world's needs, there is a collective duty to work towards addressing them as best as we can.

There's an upside to this reality: our participation can make a difference. We have the power to collaborate, influence change, and make a tangible impact.

In a world where needs continue to persist, assessing needs is an ongoing process. But this process also needs to have clear parameters. When designing your Kosher Giving Plan, you will revisit the causes that you've given to in the past and compare them with the giving opportunities currently at hand. It's a review process that you engage in from season to season, year to year, but it's not an exercise that preoccupies you from moment to moment on a 24-7 basis. The never-ending needs of the world should not overwhelm you. They should bring focus to your philanthropy and pave the path to the next pillars of kosher giving: impact, agency, and purpose.

We've opened our exploration of the pillars of kosher giving with needs, not at the expense of the other pillars, but as a reminder that good intentions and positive motivations aren't enough. Needs are a primary driver of kosher giving, moving us to act, to fix what's broken and to generate impact. But needs are also only one pillar among three. Next, we'll take a close look at the impact agents that turn philanthropic contributions into impactful actions, after which we'll get back to ourselves, developing tools to identify and define our purpose.

Kosher Food for Thought

What does your community engagement and collaboration look like? Think about your volunteer work. How can you enhance your engagement with the communities or groups you aim to support?

Are you continuously assessing and adapting your giving approach? Think about your past giving. How can you ensure your giving strategy remains responsive to changing needs?

Which needs assessment methodology are you most comfortable with? Do you take a strategic approach to determining needs or are you more reactionary in your giving, responding when called upon? What needs assessment approaches have you used, and what would you consider using in the future?

Kosher Giving Applied Actions

1. Use your Kosher Giving Journal to record your answers to the Kosher Food for Thought above.

2. **Practice data collection.** Choose a cause that's close to your heart, collect three articles of interest that further educate you about the field, and record the sources in your Kosher Giving Journal. Make sure to take notes about one critical insight from each of the articles.

3. **Create a list of needs within your community.** These can be the needs of individuals, organizations, or society at large. Record three to five causes in your Kosher Giving Journal that you have not given to in the last five years. You'll be able to draw upon these when we begin with the design of you Kosher Giving Plan.

Chapter Four

Pillar 2 - Impact Agents

The second pillar of Kosher Giving is the impact agents; the individuals, organizations, and institutions through which we give. If we're not giving directly to a beneficiary, then impact agents are a critical part of our giving. At times, they're messengers who transfer funds from donor to recipient. At times they're visionary social entrepreneurs, who develop and execute programs that address the needs that we've identified. And at times they're in the back office, overseeing the processes that make things come together seamlessly. To take our giving seriously, and to appreciate how we can give better, it's helpful to break down the different roles of impact agents and to determine whom we choose to work with.

The significance of the 'who' of giving can't be overstated. Even when we look at increasingly popular digital philanthropy platforms, the 'who' remains a central theme.

JGive, the first Israel-based online crowdfunding platform dedicated solely to philanthropic giving, hit their annual donation goal in the first month of the war alone. Serving 1,500 nonprofits with their easy-to-use online interface, they've learned a thing or two about how crowdfunding campaigns can successfully reach their fundraising goals.

We invited Yoav Well, who heads up JGive Pro, the nonprofit's premium campaigns service, to lead a session about crowdfunding at a Non-profit Accelerator program that Sector4 Strategy was running. After mapping out both the behind-the-scenes of how the campaigns work and the do-it-yourself tools that non-profits can use to launch their campaigns, Yoav paused for emphasis as he explained that "people give to people."

For all the technology, the sophistication, the speed and the streamlined visual interfaces, the secret sauce of any successful crowdfunding campaign is the human element. Whether you're asking or giving, or in many cases when you're doing a mix of both, the people engaged in the process are the most compelling case for the cause. Technology makes the process more seamless, but it works most effectively when there are people asking their friends and family to contribute to a cause that they believe in.

Think about when your niece or sibling sends you a campaign link. They're part of a team, often numbering tens to hundreds of volunteers, all mobilized to raise more funds as a collective group than any one individual could have raised on their own. They're sending you a link because they know you. This is precisely why you click, scroll to the donation field, and contribute. People don't give to technology. People give to people.

But are we, as people who give to people, on the kosher giving track to strategic planning? When the people we're giving to are intermediaries instead of direct beneficiaries, we must take a closer look at the giving chain from start to finish. Of course, we'll continue to support our niece's cause, but will that mark the full extent of our giving strategy? Should all our giving be a response to the people we know and love who reach out to us? Does this approach truly serve the needs at hand? Does it align with and advance our personal purpose? Or, put differently, is this a mindful way of giving?

Mapping the Giving Chain and Our Impact Agents

One of the most difficult aspects of kosher giving is determining who to give to. Our meaningful hearts want to give to everyone in need. But our minds remind us that we, as individuals, cannot possibly reach every single person in need.

Today, we do most of our giving indirectly, through impact agents; we tend to contribute financially to the people or the organizations that support the beneficiaries, rather than to the beneficiaries themselves.

Our goal is not to list the many forms of impact agents. Instead, we seek to provide you with the tools you need to address them mindfully. For every impact agent in the philanthropic chain, we'll provide a checklist to help you engage with these partners thoughtfully and effectively.

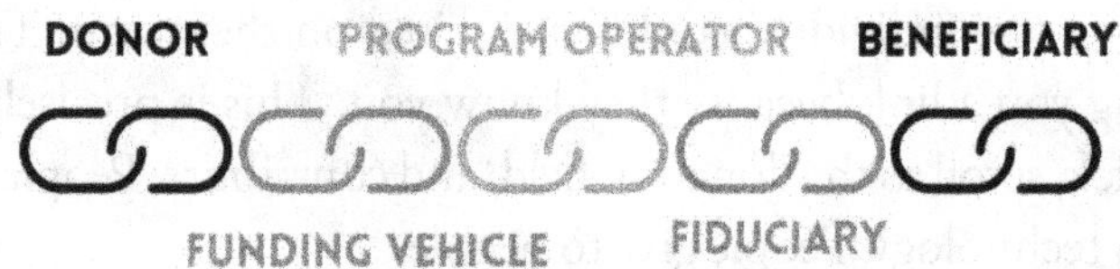

The Giving Chain

The philanthropic chain can be broken down into three types of stakeholders, linking the philanthropist to the beneficiary.

The first group of stakeholders are the funders or funding vehicles that we select. The second group includes the program operators, responsible for using the funds for their intended purpose. The third group is the fiduciary, tasked with ensuring the accountable and responsible management of the funds.

Funders

Funders and funding vehicles comprise the first category of "who" we give to. Before the programming operators receive the funding they need to perform, someone made the decision to send donor funds in their direction. These are the teams that chart the course of our charitable contributions, entrusted to reach the places where they can do the most good. They take on the responsibility of allocating the funds we give to the causes and people that need them most. Before presenting our funding checklist, the following are some examples of common types of funders that you may have worked with in the past or may consider collaborating with in the future.

Foundations

These entities often begin with strategic planning. Foundations might be private, set up by an individual or a family, or public, pooling resources from various donors. They don't typically implement programs themselves. Instead, they fund other organizations that do. By awarding grants, they support a range of initiatives, from local community projects to global humanitarian efforts. Foundations usually have specific focus areas and choose projects that align with their goals and objectives.

Grant-Making Bodies

Similar to foundations, these entities focus on distributing funds through grants. They could be part of a larger organization, a government body, or an independent entity. They evaluate proposals from various nonprofits and decide where to allocate funds based on the potential impact, feasibility, and alignment with their mission. Grant-making bodies can play an important role in supporting innovative projects and initiatives that might otherwise struggle to find funding.

Governmental Agencies

In certain cases, especially in large-scale interventions like disaster relief during the Iron Swords War, governmental agencies become primary fund distributors. They can mobilize significant resources and have the reach and authority to implement widespread programs. Israel's Social Security Agency serves as the primary conduit for funding immediate relief for displaced families and salaries for reservists. Governmental involvement in philanthropy can be complex, as it often intersects with policy-making and public administration.

Corporate Social Responsibility (CSR) Departments

In the corporate world, CSR departments oversee the distribution of a company's philanthropic funds. These can range from monetary donations to initiatives like community development projects, environmental conservation efforts, or partnerships with nonprofits. CSR programs reflect a company's commitment to social responsibility and can be a significant source of funding and support for various causes.

Each type of fund distributor brings a unique perspective and set of capabilities to the table. From the hands-on, direct approach of charity organizations to the strategic, large-scale interventions by governmental agencies and foundations, these entities span a broad spectrum of opportunities for donors and beneficiaries alike. Understanding their roles helps the kosher giving community make informed decisions about where and how to allocate our contributions, and who might be the best partners for different kinds of gifts.

It's helpful to keep the challenges that fund distributors face in mind. First, their decision-making process is a significant issue. How are they choosing which causes, among the many worthy opportunities, should receive funding? How are they sourcing the opportunities and determining who could potentially have access to their funds? What's their giving policy, and who is involved in the decision making? What is the why that defines them, the how that refines them, the 'what' that they give, and the 'who' behind the scenes?

With these considerations in mind, here's our funders checklist:

__ **Funding Priorities**: Check if their funding priorities and areas of focus match your philanthropic interests.

__ **Partnership Opportunities:** Evaluate opportunities for collaboration, co-funding, or leveraging their network and resources. Can you play a role? Will your role be meaningful and mindful?

__ **Grant-making Approach**: Understand their grant-making process, criteria for funding, and how they measure the success of their grants. This will be important for the evaluation and measurement stage of your Kosher Giving Plan.

Program Operators

Reflecting on the who of giving, we naturally gravitate towards the not-for-profit organizations, the driving forces behind positive change and activism. These entities, as their name suggests, prioritize social or environmental returns over financial gains from philanthropic investments. Not-for-profits, NGOs, or simply 'nonprofits', form the backbone of philanthropic efforts. They show up, day in and day out, to transform our aspirations into help, healing, and hope.

Non-profit organizations act as crucial bridges, transforming donor generosity into concrete, meaningful actions that meet community needs. These groups, which span from neighborhood food banks to global NGOs, utilize their strong community ties and insight into unique challenges to execute solutions that are both culturally apt and impactful. Working within limited budgets, they juggle ambitious goals with available resources, adapting to evolving needs and regulations, all while upholding donor trust and earning beneficiary respect. Their efforts turn the abstract concept of giving into tangible results, such as feeding the hungry or supplying educational materials, all while navigating the complexities of non-profit management.

Thinking of these organizations merely as functional intermediaries doesn't do justice to their role. These organizations and the people who operate them are our partners in a shared mission of making the world a little better and kinder, one act of generosity at a time.

We could give directly to recipients, but partnering with these organizations brings added value and the opportunity to amplify our contributions through their resources and expertise. Non-profits operate in a challenging environment, yet they are the kind of partners who enable us to be part of a transformative community, so long as they are reliable and effective.

Beyond non-profits, the circle of program operators includes volunteer coordinators, logistics operations, and social enterprises.

Volunteer coordinators are pivotal in managing one of the most valuable assets in the nonprofit sector: human capital. These dedicated individuals and teams are responsible for recruiting, training, and managing volunteers, ensuring that their skills and time are well-utilized.

Gitit Malka of the Paamonim organization in Israel recently explained her approach to volunteers. The organization assists 12,000 families a year in their path to financial independence. They've built their reputation of effective economic coaching through years of tried-and-true methods, and with the help of a formidable team of 3,000 highly capable and well-trained volunteers from across the country.

Gitit doesn't introduce herself as a volunteer coordinator. She is the head of the Human Resources department, overseeing their army of volunteers and equipping them with the same tools, training, and appreciation that you would expect from a corporation with a comparable number of employees. Gitit sees her role as more than a community organizer. She believes in a culture of organizational excellence that can only be attained through exceptional human capital.

When programming is focused not on human resources but on the efficiency of material resources, **Logistics and Supply Chain Managers** assume leadership roles. They are the ones who ensure that resources get to their intended destination, right and on time. They manage the complex logistics of transporting goods, from food to medical supplies, often across challenging terrains and under pressing timelines. These are the folks you want to be working with when you're shipping 10,000 bullet-proof vests across the Atlantic Ocean.

As with volunteer coordinators, these managers may or may not work within the existing framework of a non-profit organization. Shinua Chevrati, literally translated as "Social Delivery," is an example of a non-profit that has harnessed these practices, having developed a model for turning surplus into resources. They match furniture sitting unused in corporate offices, food items that aren't selling, and textiles that were expected to reach landfills, with families that need these items most. As Naava Shafner, a key player at Shinua Chevrati, describes, their noble goal is "logistics for the greater good." Through careful sourcing, efficient shipping and insightful ingenuity, their team of only 3 employees and hundreds of volunteers transforms contributions into tenfold impactful returns on investment.

When considering the rich history and heritage of program operators, **social enterprises** are a relatively new and innovative approach to social impact. These are organizations that straddle the line between traditional business and non-profit models. Their primary goal is to achieve social impact, but they do so by generating revenue. For example, a social enterprise might sell products crafted by artisans in developing countries, providing them with sustainable income while also funding development projects in their communities. Their impact is funded through the income of their business models. At times, they may forego their income due to their commitment to a cause.

My advisory firm, Sector4 Strategy, is a social enterprise. Under normal circumstances, our ongoing work with government, businesses, and the non-profit community is designed to create synergies between each of the three economic sectors. In other words, we're a business platform for generating purpose-driven impact. Naturally, in times of extreme need, such as the Iron Swords War, our team mobilized to deliver innovative value. The war's urgent needs birthed the KosherGiving.com initiative, with our leading advisors committing endless hours of voluntary service to a cause we could rally behind: promoting better giving for a vast, growing, and evolving community of donors.

One of the hallmarks of a social enterprise is that its programs and activities are infectious, drawing the direct engagement of employees and volunteers alike, much like a nonprofit. Our advisors are talented and dedicated, but we alone could not possibly have handled the volume and quality of content that the new platform was designed to deliver to the giving community. Fortunately, the value proposition was compelling, and whenever we reached out for volunteers, we had more people raise their hand than spots available to be filled. From user-experience and user-interface web development to copywriting, from editorial and advisory board roles to social media management, Sector4 has succeeded in delivering KosherGiving.com to a wide audience thanks to the dedication of volunteers who appreciate the social impact of our work.

Although social enterprises are like nonprofits in their ability to enlist volunteers, they are held to a different financial performance standard. As a business, Sector4 will need to develop marketplace valued services to keep KosherGiving.com and its associated programs alive and to ensure sustainability. Our volunteers are not taken for granted, and, as such, we will continue to invest in the platform by creating revenue streams that allow us to compensate our exceptional, dedicated team members. As impact agents, we align causes and purpose, while being mindful of innovative opportunities to create partnerships both within the organization and with the broader public.

So, how can we best choose the best program operators to partner with? Here's a checklist:

__ **Make sure your missions are aligned**: Ensure their mission and activities align with your philanthropic goals and values. As we explore values, visions, missions, and goals in the next chapter, keep in mind that our giving purpose should be in sync with that of our program operators.

__ **Check out their track record:** Assess each operator's past projects and outcomes to gauge their effectiveness and impact.

__ Don't compromise on **operational transparency**: Look for clear communication, financial transparency, and accountability in their operations. Keep this in mind, as we address the subjects of trust and integrity.

Fiduciaries

Fiduciaries are a cornerstone upon which the integrity of the philanthropic process rests. A fiduciary, in its broadest sense, is an individual or organization entrusted to manage assets or funds for the benefit of others, holding a legal and ethical responsibility to act in the best interest of the beneficiaries. In philanthropy, fiduciaries are the guardians of donors' intentions, ensuring that contributions are managed and utilized with the utmost care and responsibility.

Fiduciaries in philanthropy, including trustees of charitable trusts or foundations, financial advisors, legal advisors, and complianc e officers, each fulfill essential roles in managing charitable resources. Trustees oversee operations and decision-making, aligning with the organization's mission and donor intentions. Financial advisors balance fund growth and risk, ensuring asset preservation and productivity for philanthropic endeavors. Legal advisors navigate charity and tax laws, ensuring compliance and maintaining organizational integrity. Auditors and compliance officers uphold transparency and accountability, regularly reviewing and auditing financial practices to meet the highest standards of integrity an d efficiency.

Fiduciaries face a series of challenges that require a delicate balance between competing values and priorities. They need to navigate the complexities of investment management, ensuring that the funds grow while being readily available for philanthropic purposes. They must stay abreast of changing legal and regulatory landscapes, adapting strategies to ensure compliance and maximize impact. And most critically, they must maintain the delicate balance between the philanthropic mission and the practicalities of financial management, ensuring that the organization's goals are achieved without compromising ethical standards or donor intent.

Last month I was invited to weigh in on a set of not-so-comfortable discussions among the Members of a nonprofit organization's Executive Board. The Board Members were at odds about how and when to allocate funds to a grantee organization. In the world of US-originating donations to Israel, these are common questions.

The "American Friends of" organization is a US registered nonprofit, dedicated to supporting a cause or set of causes in Israel. As a funding organization, they are tasked with moving funds that were raised to beneficiary organizations in Israel. As a fiduciary, accountable to regulators and donors alike, they need to ensure that the transfer of funds complies with best practices and regulations. But compliance isn't always a precise science, and boards need to agree on internal policy to function effectively.

Unfortunately, I was called in when the situation had long been broken. It turned out that the "American Friends of" organization hadn't sent any funds to the Israeli beneficiary in three years. They had millions of dollars sitting in their accounts, effectuating none of the change that the donors anticipated. Beyond the obvious and outrageous functional impasse, the irony was that some of the board thought that it was their fiduciary responsibility to withhold the transfer of funds.

Here's the clarifying point: fiduciaries need to balance more than one set of values. In this case, one value is the proper management of funds, and the other value is generating impact. Importantly, both values support donors and beneficiaries alike, as everyone benefits from accountability, and everyone benefits from positive project outcomes. As such, balancing these values isn't easy. Yes, a board member who is concerned that insufficient reporting has been submitted to justify a transfer of funds needs to take action, whether by requesting further information to investigate the situation or working closely with the beneficiary to resolve issues of concern. But by focusing on procedure alone, without working collaboratively to see to it that those funds are indeed transferred in a timely fashion, that fiduciary is no longer fulfilling their role as the donor's representative and impact agent.

Fortunately, this organization is back on track. They've clarified their policies internally and with their affiliates, they've processed the paperwork, and their new Executive Board is improving their interpersonal dynamics. But feelings were hurt in the process, and not all the dedicated, selfless, thoughtful volunteers who have been the lifeblood of the organization for years will continue volunteering. It's a set of circumstances that can be avoided with clear role definitions and agreed upon expectations.

To both appreciate the role of fiduciaries and to plan mindfully, here's a helpful checklist you can use:

__ **Financial Expertise and Stewardship**: Ensure they have a strong track record in managing funds responsibly and effectively.

__ **Alignment with Philanthropic Objectives**: Their strategies should align with your philanthropic vision and long-term goals.

__ **Regulatory Compliance and Risk Management**: Confirm their adherence to legal and ethical standards, and ability to manage financial risks. This is what they're there for. Let's make sure that they've got this.

Agency for Greater Efficiency

Impact agents are one part donor representative, one part agent of change. As philanthropists, we anticipate that they will translate the resources entrusted to them into action. As such, we anticipate that they will be able to create efficiencies that we, on our own, cannot. These can manifest as:

Streamlined operations: Effective impact agents operate according to streamlined processes, ensuring that the maximum amount of resources reaches their intended causes. They focus on minimizing administrative costs and overhead, thus enhancing the direct impact of the funds.

Transparent communication: They prioritize clear and regular communication with donors and stakeholders. This transparency in reporting fund allocation, project progress, and impact informs donors about how their contributions are making a difference, building trust.

Strategic allocation: Impact agents are tasked with the strategic allocation of resources. They ensure that funds are directed towards areas where they can have the most significant impact, aligning with the goals and needs of each recipient community.

Collaborative approaches: They foster collaboration among various entities to pool resources and expertise. Doing so helps stakeholders leverage their strengths, while avoiding the duplication of efforts, and enhancing the overall impact of philanthropic activities.

Impact-driven execution: Their focus is on creating tangible, measurable impact, ensuring that donated funds translate into real, positive changes in the community.

Adaptive and responsive behavior: Impact agents need to be adaptable to changing circumstances and responsive to emerging needs. Their ability to quickly adjust their strategies ensures that interventions remain relevant and effective.

Efficiency is not easily managed in times of crisis or war. Extreme circumstances may be grounds for temporarily limited efficiencies, but they remain the goal and challenge us to refine and recalibrate whenever possible. That said, by following the above frame of reference, the path toward mindful kosher giving will be much more straightforward.

Impact Agent Thresholds: Trust, Integrity, and Accountability

While efficiencies can be compromised, trust and integrity cannot. Trust and integrity are the bedrocks of effective philanthropy. They ensure that the philanthropic process is not only effective but also respected and valued by all parties involved - donors, impact agents, and beneficiaries.

Trust in philanthropy is cultivated through consistent, transparent actions and ethical conduct across all parties, engaging everyone from donors to impact agents to beneficiaries. It's sustained by showing how funds are responsibly managed and used, and by the tangible outcomes of philanthropic work. Here, integrity is key—it's staying true to our moral compass, being candid about what's possible, and responsibly overseeing resources. When trust and integrity intertwine, they create a philanthropic environment where efficiency meets respect, ensuring that every stakeholder is treated with dignity.

A Word About Fees

While efficiency in philanthropy dictates that resources are used effectively, integrity ensures that these resources are employed in an ethical and transparent manner.

Often, operational costs are used as a measure of these elements, but this approach merits closer examination.

There are legitimate concerns regarding fees in philanthropy, especially when high operational costs might imply less money reaching those in need. Donors often scrutinize these costs, seeking assurance that their contributions are used for their intended purposes.

Philanthropic impact agents - large foundations and online platforms alike - face real costs in meeting donor expectations. These include staffing, program execution, and maintaining operational infrastructure, all of which are essential for delivering impactful results. These operational costs may be necessary for maintaining the quality and sustainability of philanthropic efforts.

Minimizing unnecessary expenses in philanthropy is key, but it's just as important to recognize the worth of professional management. Transparent communication about these costs helps donors understand the complexities involved in effectively managing philanthropic funds and operations. This understanding fosters an appreciation for the intricate balance required to make a meaningful impact.

Who We Give Through

Often, the question of who we give to is a question of who we give *through*. When it comes to kosher giving, the way our contributions are handled is as important as the act of giving itself. We want to make sure that our donations not only reach their intended destinations, but that they do so in a manner that aligns with our values and the principles of ethical stewardship. To do so, we must work closely with the people who oversee the ethical management of funds, the fund distributors who allocate resources, and the program operators who turn financial contributions into real-world impact.

While fiduciaries, fund distributors, and program operators play crucial roles in philanthropy, they may not always suffice independently. Each specializes in specific aspects of the philanthropic process, yet there remains a need for comprehensive guidance and strategic planning. Their functions, primarily focused on managing and implementing philanthropic efforts, might not encompass the broader perspective required for holistic philanthropic strategy. At times, a more comprehensive approach is needed.

Advisors serve a fundamentally different role than the impact agents described above. Their advisors provide strategic guidance, helping donors navigate the complex landscape of philanthropy. They bring a bird's-eye view, offering insights that span across various aspects of giving, from selecting causes to measuring impact. The beauty of advisory and strategic planning lies in its ability to bring coherence and direction to the philanthropic process. It's about connecting the dots between the donors' intentions, the capabilities of fiduciaries and fund distributors, and the on-the-ground realities faced by program operators.

Sector4 Strategy is a social enterprise, as noted earlier in this chapter, but our primary mode of operation is providing advisory services to stakeholders across the giving chain, from philanthropists to funders to program operators to fiduciaries. Going forward, we'll take a closer look at the role of advisors and how we can accompany you on your philanthropic journey. For now, it's worth noting that advisors are part of the impact agency community, even as we serve a broader function.

Impact agents are the second pillar upon which we'll be able to design and substantiate our giving plans. With the needs at the forefront and the impact agents serving beneficiaries and donors alike, it's time we take a closer look at the third pillar of giving: ourselves.

Kosher Food for Thought

What experiences have you had with impact agents? Have they met your expectations in terms of efficiency and impact?

How do you define trust and integrity? What are the qualities you seek in an impact agency partner? Which impact agents do you trust most?

Try to assess costs in comparison with value: Reflect on the costs associated with your philanthropic activities, including those for operational services. Or consider the cost of this book. How do you view these factors in terms of their influence on the impact of your philanthropic efforts?

Kosher Giving Applied Actions

1. Use your Kosher Giving Journal to record your answers to the Kosher Food for Thought above.

2. Create a short list of the top three to five program operators with whom you enjoy working.

3. Review your giving over the past three years and create a list of the partners and organizations you work with to fund projects. While you're at it, include the sums that you've contributed to each cause (this will help you prepare for your Kosher Giving Plan).

Chapter Five

Pillar 3 - Purpose

In times of conflict, such as the ongoing Iron Swords Hamas-Israel War, the Israeli community rushes to rally behind its soldiers, often by sending boxes of food as a gesture of support. Tali Tabib, who lost her son Omer in the 2021 Guardian of the Walls operation, embraced the same approach when she founded Alumot B'Omer, an Israeli registered non-profit, that same year. The organization was geared towards supporting soldiers, aligning with conventional wisdom. "Omer had an innate sense of what people needed, and he acted on it," Tali says. Now, she's steering Alumot B'Omer in a new direction, shifting the focus to support bereaved families.

It was a week into the war when Tali Tabib and I spoke about her pivot. We were on a Zoom call when she said that she was at the most special place in the world. She turned the self-facing camera so that the gravesite of her son, Omer, came into focus.

Omer Tabib was a young man of extraordinary kindness, and he was unusually perceptive. "The joy he received from giving was all the reward he needed," Tali says, her words making it easy to envision the kind of person Omer was. It was Omer's nature that prompted Tali to look beyond the obvious and consider overlooked needs, exacerbated by a war unlike any preceding military campaigns.

While support for soldiers on the battlefield is critical and meaningful, Tali and her team of volunteers at Alumot B'Omer understand that this war calls for something more — something that not many were paying attention to. "I know what it's like," Tali reflected. "The families of the civilians and soldiers who fell are broken apart. I know what it takes to get through that. But I had something that they don't have. My son Omer was the only fallen Israeli soldier in Operation Guardians of the Wall. I had the entire country standing with me and supporting me. But this, this is different. These families are alone."

To address this gap, Alumot B'Omer repositioned its efforts to serve the grieving families, away from the spotlight, squarely where they were needed most. Instead of solely focusing on soldiers, they expanded their scope. Tali explains: "Just like we previously identified soldiers who needed financial help, we are now focusing on bereaved families and providing support according to their specific needs." The methodology, the volunteer team and the operations all adapted to a new mission, and a new purpose.

When everyone else was rushing to the front-lines, raising funds for everything from Bamba snacks to boxers for soldiers, Tali and the Alumot B'Omer volunteers started with the home front. They found the families that were mourning the horrific loss of their loved ones, some for individual victims and others for entire families. In all cases, Alumot B'Omer did what Omer did best: they matched the support to the need.

Through Alumot B'Omer, Tali has managed to blend her personal loss with a collective sense of duty, creating a legacy for Omer that echoes and resonates throughout the Israeli community. Tali is driven both by the memory of her son and by her new sense of purpose.

Purpose is a combination of meaningful giving and directional focus. It's comprised of our values and the roles that we fill to advance those values. By tracking our pivots, we can look at our purpose from the outside-in, defining what's important to us by discovering where we choose to point the spotlight.

Pivots

Tali's pivot from supporting soldiers to supporting bereaved families was not driven by data analysis, group surveys, or community-wide interviews to assess needs and build a plan of action. Tali asked herself, "What's my role? What can I contribute?" Looking inward, she sought guidance to shape her actions towards others.

The journey of introspection and self-analysis, as Tali experienced, can be intuitive and natural. Her profound experiences as a bereaved mother deeply influenced her thoughts and actions, leading her swiftly and decisively. Yet, for many, this process unfolds more gradually, involving several shifts and adjustments along the way.

The Israel Heart2Heart organization is a good example. They, too, pivoted over the course of this war. In their case, they pivoted twice.

Rabbi Chaim Slavaticki from Fort Lauderdale and businessman Eric Donner from Boca Raton founded the organization. They noticed that IDF veterans were returning from sponsored trips to the US with temporary relief but no long-term support. They asked, "What happens after they go back to Israel?" The answer lay in a continuous, supportive-care process that they established for cohorts of 20 veterans at a time. From yoga sessions that span the country's geography to life skill workshops and expert-led seminars, the program's reach is extensive and impactful.

When the normal rhythm of life was disrupted on October 7, 2023, Israel Heart2Heart made their first pivot, establishing a 'war room' to organize crucial support. A swift fundraising initiative amassed $250,000, underscoring the Israel Heart2Heart community's solidarity and generosity. These funds were directed to the most pressing needs, supplying equipment to soldiers, and providing economic support to families bearing the war's brunt.

Several of the IDF veterans from the Israel Heart2Heart program were enlisted in the reserves, filling roles that allowed them to serve and restore personal dignity. As the pace of ongoing programming shifted and with an outpouring of community support, this first pivot to address national needs was well received. The organization's war room, a hub of ongoing activity, became the focal point for distributing resources. However, the new logistics operation presented new challenges, such as navigating the clearing of customs at Ben Gurion Airport to ensure that vital supplies like clothing, hygiene products, and tactical gear reached those in nee d.

The Adopt-a-Family program was another program that reflected Israel Heart2Heart's adaptability. Recognizing the upheaval families experienced, whether through displacement or loss, the organization provided a bridge between those willing to give and those in need. It was another necessary and time-sensitive adaptation, but it was temporary.

Shmil Atlas, Executive Director of Israel Heart2Heart, anticipates a rise in PTSD cases amongst veterans both during and after the current war. The surge in charitable giving during the conflict might wane, but the need for comprehensive PTSD support will only intensify. Shmil, along with Rabbi Slavaticki, Eric Donner, and the board, began pivoting back to their core mission and purpose to better position themselves to meet this long-term need.

Tali Tabib's pivot with Alumot B'Omer and Israel Heart2Heart's shift during the Iron Swords War represent two distinct types of purpose-driven pivots. Tali's change was deeply personal, redefining her life purpose in response to profound personal and national loss. Her shift to supporting bereaved families marked a redirection of her mission, driven by her own experiences and internal reflection.

In contrast, Israel Heart2Heart's pivots were temporary, strategically adapting to immediate needs before ultimately returning to their core mission. Their temporary shift to immediate war-related needs and subsequent refocusing on their primary mission of supporting veterans with PTSD demonstrates organizational ability, while staying true to their foundational purpose.

Both cases are instructive as we explore the third pillar of kosher giving: individual and organizational purpose. Some pivots are circumstantial, but those are not the focus of this chapter. When pivots are an expression of essential inner meaning, they demonstrate intentional purpose. At times, transformative and at times strategically flexible pivots can reveal what we care about most.

Values

For an individual, discovering purpose in life often involves a journey of introspection and reflection. This journey includes identifying core values, passions, and strengths, and then aligning them with actions and decisions. When your purpose aligns with your giving, your philanthropy becomes more than just a series of donations. It manifests as an expression of your deepest values and convictions, while infusing your contributions with deeper meaning and personal fulfillment.

If purpose in life is a driving force that, when unlocked, can serve as your guiding light, then organizational purpose can do the same for a foundation, non-profit, business, or even a government agency. Just as individual purpose is shaped by personal values and experiences, an organization's purpose is crafted from its collective mission, vision, and core values. This purpose becomes the guide for its operations, informing its decision-making process, as well as its strategies and initiatives. Purpose helps organizations stay focused and aligned with their fundamental goals, ensuring that their actions and impacts resonate deeply with their foundational ethos and the needs they aim to address.

Organizations rigorously analyze values, vision, mission, goals, and objectives to define their purpose, and individuals can mirror this process in philanthropy. It calls for deep reflection on core values and beliefs, envisioning the long-term impact desired and setting clear, achievable goals. Defining a personal mission paves a focused, purpose-driven philanthropic path. This structured approach aligns giving with personal beliefs, ensuring its strategic, impactful, and true to your identity and aspirations.

Defining personal values is highly individual. Here are some general guidelines we can use to begin to define the values we hold dear:

Engage in **thoughtful introspection**, considering life experiences where you felt deeply satisfied or notably dissatisfied. Reflecting on these moments can reveal underlying values that are important to you.

Determine which aspects of life hold the greatest significance for you. **Identify and rank your values** in order of importance, focusing on non-negotiables.

Seek out sources of inspiration. Look towards individuals who inspire you, whether they're personal acquaintances or public figures. Understand the values they embody and how these align with your aspirations.

Practice journaling or mind mapping to explore and connect your thoughts. Writing down your ideas or creating visual representations can clarify and solidify your values. You can use your Kosher Giving Journal for this.

Regularly **reassess your values**, acknowledging that they may change as you grow and encounter new experiences. This ongoing process ensures that your values remain relevant and true to your current self.

Each of these approaches offers a unique way to explore and articulate the values that guide your decisions and actions, including your approach to philanthropy. However, it is the last approach, the one that invites us to re-evaluate our values, which reminds us that our values are not set in stone. What happens when our values change? What about when our values clash, or when we need to choose which one takes precedence over others? How do these changes influence the decisions we make? How do they affect our giving?

Metuka Benjamin, internationally recognized educator, social entrepreneur and Advisory Board Member of KosherGiving.com, called the other day. We discussed giving trends during the war and her upcoming meeting with a philanthropist regarding an innovative program to empower young Israel-supporting adults on North American college campuses. During our conversation, she emphasized the unpredictability of donor priorities.

This point was illustrated by a past fundraising experience for Connect Israel, an organization that Metuka founded. This initiative fosters leadership among young adults in the U.S. and Israel, encouraging collaboration between the two groups. Metuka had confidently expected support from a philanthropist she knew well, especially considering a previous multi-million-dollar donation to the Steven S. Wise schools she established in Los Angeles.

She was shocked by his response: "We're not giving to Israeli causes now. We don't like the Israeli government's policies."

The donor reassured Metuka that it was nothing personal. They valued her, and they valued her work, but not enough to drive them to contribute to the new cause. However, other values came into play, taking precedence over the initial expectations.

Metuka was curious: "I wonder what she's thinking now, during the war. I can't imagine that she would avoid giving to Israel."

We didn't discuss the name of the family foundation, and I am unaware of their philanthropic choices in the current situation. But, as Metuka and I can attest, the values of a philanthropist or organization change. And even when they don't, the relative weight that we attribute to one value may shift as we consider how it compares to others.

This situation mirrors what occurred with the Achim LaNeshek organization in Israel. In the months before the war, they organized high-profile protests against the Israeli government over judicial reform. Known for mobilizing supporters to sign letters and vow not to serve in IDF reserves as a form of protest, their stance shifted dramatically when war broke out in Israel, leading to a change in their approach.

The protests came to an end. Everyone showed up for reserve duty. And the organization channeled their resources to support a wide range of initiatives, both civilian and military. Was it a change of heart? Did their values shift drastically? Was it the sheer force of circumstance?

Values can change, but values are not to be confused with trends. Values are fundamental components of our identity that evolve as we endure significant life experiences and engage in introspection. While it's natural for values to undergo refinement or shift in focus, such changes typically occur gradually and meaningfully, not whimsically or suddenly. This evolution is supposed to reflect our growth and adaptation to new understandings and circumstances.

The challenge for the philanthropist is two-fold. First, we need to determine what our values are and articulate them as best we can. Second, we need to consider whether a shift in our giving represents a change in values, or in the roles that we choose to fill.

Roles

Once an organization—be it private, public, or non-profit—has successfully defined its values, the leadership proceeds by determining its vision, mission, goals, and objectives. Whether the philanthropist chooses to follow the same regimen or develop their approach informally, it's important that values are expressed in terms of roles.

Our purpose answers existential questions like "Why are we here?" or "What's our role?" For organizational funders, the big question is about how they can put available resources to best use, while for individual donors it's about how they can make their giving meaningful.

These three pillars - needs, impact agents, and purpose - each have distinct focuses. Needs concern the beneficiaries, purpose revolves around the giver, and impact agents are the connectors. If we use the common organizational language noted above, then vision is an expression of our values as givers; goals and objectives focus on the recipient's needs; and mission is the role that we intend to fill.

Roles define our unique position in the philanthropic ecosystem. Understanding our roles ensures our philanthropic actions are both personally rewarding and effectively targeted, aligning our financial, intellectual, or network capacities with areas where we can make the most impact. Accordingly, we might define the role of organizational funders as the position responsible for strategizing resource utilization to address specific issues, while the role of individual donors is to seek personal alignment with their giving.

As challenging as it may be to define our values, determining our kosher giving roles can be even more difficult. As the connective tissue between the values that drive us and our capacity for impact, our roles are often influenced by external factors. The process of finding our stride is interactive and experiential, involving needs assessment, interactions with impact agents, and active engagement in giving. Our roles make our purpose practical, even as they evolve through experiences, trials, and adjustments.

Prepared for the Journey

Yes, it's time to build upon the pillars of giving. Up to now, we've laid the groundwork for philanthropy. We've covered meaningful, mindful, and measurable giving and examined our pillars: starting with needs, then impact agents, and now exploring our purpose. Each element is essential, and together, they serve as our starting point. This is where the journey of giving truly begins.

Armed with these building blocks, it's time to dive in. We're transitioning from laying the foundation to constructing the framework. We'll craft your Kosher Giving Plan and start putting it into action. Make sure to bring everything we've gathered so far — we're about to shift gears and enter a new phase of our philanthropic journey.

Kosher Food for Thought

How do your core values influence your philanthropic activities? Can you cite specific instances where your values directly shaped your giving?

In what ways have you identified and embraced your unique role in philanthropy? How has this understanding of your role changed your approach to giving?

How does your personal or organizational purpose align with your philanthropic actions? Can you describe how this purpose has guided your decisions and strategies in giving?

Kosher Giving Applied Actions

1. Use your Kosher Giving Journal to record your answers to the Kosher Food for Thought above.

2. Create a mind map. Use the open canvas in your Kosher Giving Journal to express your thinking about your personal values. On the following page, use the designated space to list up to 10 of your leading values.

3. Craft a vision statement. Write one concise sentence that will serve as your self-inspiring call to better giving.

4. List two to three goals that describe how you want to improve your philanthropic efforts over the next 12 months.

Part 2: Perspectives That Shape Our Giving Mindset and Strategic Commitment

Chapter Six

A Traditional Frame of Mind to Inform Your Next Steps

In some ways, giving is simple and straightforward. We contribute resources to fill a need, and then we move on to the next project. Yet, even at its most fundamental level and when executed with efficiency, there exist underlying elements that shape not just the transaction, but the deeper relationship between giver and recipient.

Moses ben Maimon (1138–1204), commonly known as Maimonides and also referred to by the acronym Rambam, was a philosopher, astronomer, prince, thought leader, physician to kings, rabbi, and codifier of Jewish law and ethical principles. He undertook to systematically map out "kosher" guidelines for Torah-observant Jews in every field of life. Included among these is philanthropy, where his guidelines are as universally relevant as his teachings in philosophy, science, and medicine.

In the 10th and final chapter of his teachings concerning gifts for the poor, Maimonides presents an eight-level framework for his approach to practical giving. The enduring relevance of these guidelines, centuries after they were written, reveals much about the consistent nature of human psychology, and offers valuable insights into enhancing our approach to philanthropy.

At first glance, the framework is linear, with one rung of the ladder outranking the rung beneath. But a closer look reveals not only different levels of virtue, but different dimensions of the giving experience as well.

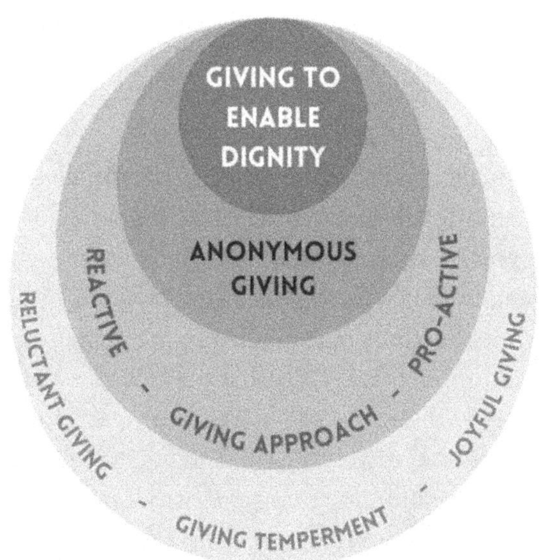

Maimonides Levels of Giving

Your Giving Disposition

According to Maimonides, the most basic levels of giving are a study in our personal disposition when giving, as reflected in the interaction between the donor and the recipient. This dimension is a comparison between 'reluctant giving' with 'joyful giving.'

Reluctant giving often stems from social pressure or obligation, rather than from a genuine interest in the cause or person. Imagine donating at an event to a cause that doesn't resonate with you or giving to someone living on the street out of unease, rather than from a place of true empathy. This type of uncomfortable but necessary giving is the most basic form of philanthropy. It may lack the depth of heartfelt giving, feeling more transactional. Yet, it's an essential first step in the philanthropic journey, opening our eyes to others' needs. It's important not to shun reluctant giving but to view it as a gateway to more profound, fulfilling forms of generosity.

In contrast, joyful giving focuses less on the gift's size and more on the genuine enthusiasm behind it. It's seen in simple acts, like baking for a neighbor or a child sharing their lunch—small deeds laden with emotional significance, reflecting a true wish to help. This giving enriches both giver and receiver, fostering empathy and gratitude, and leaving the receiver feeling genuinely valued. Joyful giving, with its heartfelt nature, outranks reluctant giving, even when comparing a reluctant gift that provides for all the needs of the beneficiary with a joyful gift that only provides for some of the needs. The superior attitude of joyful giving is a celebration of the spirit of sharing, reinforcing that generosity's true value lies in the intention, not the amount.

Taking Initiative in Giving

These first two levels of giving are about interpersonal interaction. The next two levels are about taking initiative.

Reactive giving, level three, is a common and sincere response to immediate needs. It often occurs when approached for fundraising or when a charity you've supported asks for help. This giving is crucial, especially in urgent situations like natural disasters, unexpected emergencies, or regional crises. Reactive giving is about timely support, being part of a responsive system ready to act when needed.

Proactive giving, the next level, takes a more forward-thinking approach. It involves recognizing and addressing needs within your community or sphere of influence before they are explicitly voiced. This form of giving requires a deeper level of engagement and awareness of the world around you. For example, a business leader might proactively create a scholarship fund, recognizing the need for educational support long before potential beneficiaries consider applying for support.

Proactive giving also plays a crucial role in addressing systemic issues that may not always be in the immediate public eye, such as mental health, social inequalities, and environmental concerns. Pre-emptively identifying and addressing these challenges through proactive giving works to prevent problems, paving the way for long-term, sustainable solutions.

These first four levels of giving—reluctant, joyful, reactive, and proactive—guide our personal giving approach by characterizing our attentiveness to needs and our interactions with beneficiaries. The next types of giving, outlined below, differ as they focus on the absence of a relationship between the giver and the recipient.

Dignity in Giving

Maimonides' framework for anonymous giving reveals a profound respect for the recipient's dignity. He introduces three levels of anonymity in giving, each with its unique impact on both the giver and the receiver.

The first tier of anonymous giving, or level five in Maimonides' full framework, involves donors not knowing the recipients of their aid. For example, a donor might establish a foundation and de-

liberately remain uninformed about its beneficiaries. This method preserves the recipients' dignity and independence, removing the dynamic of a direct, personal relationship with the donor. Such giving fosters a culture of respect within the community, where the focus is on a collective benefit, rather than on an individual's needs
.

The next level is best described by the extreme yet instructive story of Yossele, the Holy Miser who lived in Poland in the 17th century. Yossele seemed stingy, yet he was secretly a generous benefactor. He meticulously maintained his public image to keep his acts of kindness hidden, ensuring that those he helped never knew of his involvement. This level of anonymous giving challenges the giver to embrace a form of altruism which sidesteps recognition and focuses only on the benefit of the beneficiary.

The highest level of anonymous giving, as Maimonides outlines, is the double-blind method where neither the giver nor the recipient knows the other's identity. Today, this can be achieved through trusted online platforms where donations are made and distributed anonymously.

Such giving strips away any cause for direct gratitude, focusing purely on the act of helping and the communal good it serves. It upholds the utmost dignity and respect for both parties, nurturing a culture of unconditional generosity and shared impact.

As noble as anonymity is, there is one more level of giving that, according to Maimonides, surpasses them all. This level doesn't require us to be hidden from the recipient, nor is it limited to proactive or reactive perspectives. It may not even require us to smile.

The eighth level is in a league of its own.

Redefining Giving

Maimonides' highest level of giving transcends the act of charity and focuses on empowering recipients to become self-sufficient.

This form of giving is about providing people with the means and opportunities to stand on their own, rather than simply addressing their immediate needs.

It involves actions like a business owner offering employment to those struggling to find work or providing interest-free loans to cash-strapped individuals with viable business.

This level of philanthropy creates partnerships, nurtures potential, and respects the dignity and aspirations of each recipient. It's not just about alleviating need, but aims to eradicate it by investing in people's untapped capabilities. It equips individuals with the tools they need for sustained independence and success. In this model, the traditional roles of giver and recipient blur, as everyone becomes a participant in a mutually beneficial relationship.

This approach contributes to collective outcomes and redefines dignity through empowering actions, creating a win-win scenario for all who are involved.

Imagine a scenario where your contributions consistently lead to meaningful and lasting outcomes. Imagine that each investment not only fulfilled immediate needs but also seeded new opportunities for growth. Imagine that the people you worked with weren't third-party intermediaries or end-user beneficiaries, but vested partners with whom you share a vision, inspiration, and sense of commitment.

Shaping Our Perspectives on Well-Aligned Giving

Maimonides' initial seven levels of giving encompass three dimensions: our personal disposition to giving, our methods for identifying giving opportunities, and our commitment to preserving the recipient's dignity. Together, they add a degree of qualitative depth to the 3 M's of meaningful, mindful and measurable kosher giving and the corresponding 3 pillars of purpose, impact agents and needs. These dimensions are instrumental in steering us towards understanding the essence, rather than just the mechanics, of well-aligned giving.

As we begin designing our Kosher Giving Plan, we'll see how our 3 pillars can be well aligned, but not without keeping Maimonides' perspectives in mind.

As important as clarity will be for our Kosher Giving Plan, "aligned giving" is not limited to the columns of our workbook corresponding with each other. Alignment can be found in each and every act of generosity.

Before we take a bird's-eye view of our personal giving landscape, let's remember that we may give differently in different situations, and that every giving opportunity is an opportunity for mutual giver-recipient growth.

And let's keep the pinnacle of Maimonides' ideal giving approach in mind as well. Giving not through gifts, but by establishing partnerships is aligned giving at its best.

This means that we consider how multiple resources and needs could align in different ways that may break the traditional molds of donor and recipient. In doing so, we can pave a path towards innovative partnership models that we'll discuss in Part 4 of this book, as we continue the design and execution of your 4-Step Kosher Giving Plan.

Kosher Food for Thought

Evaluate your giving temperament. How do joy and reluctance appear in your giving? What was the most joyful gift you've given in the last three months?

Are you a proactive donor or a reactive giver? Have you found yourself anticipating needs before they are explicitly presented? Are these anticipated needs part of your regular giving routine, or do they represent new opportunities for you to explore?

How important is anonymity to you as a donor? Do you prefer giving directly or indirectly? When was your giving the most rewarding to you? When was it most rewarding to the beneficiary?

Kosher Giving Applied Actions

1. Use your Kosher Giving Journal to record your answers to the Kosher Food for Thought above.

2. Make a list of the gifts that you gave with a smile. What fraction of your giving do they represent? Set a goal for increasing that number, either by changing your mindset or by giving more frequently to causes that make you feel joyful.

3. Envision partnerships. Think of one person who you could better support by providing them with the means to make themselves more successful. Set a goal, record it, and commit to taking steps to ensure its realization.

Chapter Seven

Your Intentional Commitment to Strategic Giving

We've explored the principles of kosher giving. We've described needs, impact agents and purpose, the three pillars essential to effective philanthropy. However, to truly bring this framework to life, a conscious decision is required. You'll need to prioritize strategic giving over casual or convenient forms of giving.

Do you give socially? Have you been motivated by the giving tendencies of your social circle or community? Social giving, which involves contributing to causes valued by those around us, bolsters community ties and a shared sense of purpose. Its merits lie in strengthening communal bonds and jointly tackling issues. But should all our giving be social?

What about giving based upon familiarity with a cause or fundraiser? This often involves geographical or relational proximity to a need. It might include donations to local charities or helping people in your immediate network. This proximity-based giving allows for a personal connection and a clear understanding of the impact. But should all our giving be based upon what we already know about?

These forms of generosity are in line with reactionary giving, Maimonides' third level of giving, as described in the previous chapter. While these accessible forms of giving fulfill immediate needs and resonate within our community, they may not fully embrace broader needs or fulfill our deeper philanthropic purpose.

To genuinely address the full spectrum of needs and align with our purpose, we must evolve beyond convenient or 'easy-access' giving. By committing ourselves to a giving strategy that reflects our values and goals, our giving rises to the level of proactive philanthropy, contributing to meaningful, mindful, and measurable impact (and change).

As we'll discover in the coming chapters, this is not an either-or situation. You'll have the opportunity to decide how much of your giving portfolio is methodically planned and how much allows for flexibility. You might find that social giving, for instance, isn't just a casual choice but an integral part of your strategy, allocating a specific budget range for such opportunities.

Your approach to giving will be dynamic, capable of adapting to changing circumstances. What sets it apart from easy-access giving is that it offers structure, the ability to track your impact, and the basis for personal and purposeful growth over time.

Paradigm Shift: From Convenience to Strategy

When mother-daughter team Ginnie and Sarah Johnson came to Ariel, they were driven to build a strategic framework. Ginnie had been involved in supporting the city for two decades. When she and Sarah co-founded King's Daughters, a social business "celebrating women & girls as King's Daughters with truth and beauty," they wanted a percentage of their earnings to be directed toward causes in Israel. This was a fundamental part of their business, and it deserved the same degree of planning that they were dedicating to marketing, sales, and development.

Ginnie and Sarah flew from Dallas to Israel and spent the greater part of a week in Ariel. I introduced them to tens of projects across the city, in the fields of education, the golden age, the arts, science, and more. Their hands-on study and experience led the dynamic duo to develop an extensive portfolio of projects worthy of the support of their business and, at trade shows and events, their customers. They created a unifying theme for 26 different projects, each corresponding to one of the letters of the alphabet. Between Sarah's videography and web development skills and Ginnie's works of visual art, their articulation and presentation of the projects was breathtaking and compelling.

Ginnie and Sarah were purposeful and proactive. They resolved to give mindfully, and they travelled thousands of miles to meet impact agents—from program operators to funding vehicles—in person. And they created a measurable giving plan that was carefully interwoven with their business plan.

For Ginnie and Sarah, strategic giving was an intentional decision directly related to the establishment of a new, ambitious, and purposeful business. But there are people for whom strategy marks all their giving. For these thoughtful philanthropists, every project is a careful study.

Lowell Milken is a strategic philanthropist. He has funded schools, higher education initiatives, sports centers, the arts, and more in Ariel, for over four decades. Judging by the number of projects he's contributed to, it would seem as though Lowell's commitment to the city is either undiscerning or unconditional. But if that were the case, it doesn't explain his tendency to challenge giving opportunities with numerous thoughtful and discerning questions.

Ron Nachman, the late founder and longstanding mayor of Ariel, established a steadfast relationship with Lowell. For all the qualities that Ron would attribute to the philanthropist that he held in the highest regard, he found Lowell's inquisitive nature to be exceptional. When Ron primed me for my meetings with Lowell, he would always stress the need to be thoroughly prepared, not only to deliver a presentation, but to answer all forms of questions as well.

Lowell is not just a philanthropist; he's invested in understanding every aspect of a project. He delves into the needs, solutions, long-term plans, and financial details. His commitment comes only after gaining confidence in his partners' dedication and capability, ensuring the project aligns with his vision for impact.

His purposeful strategy runs wide and deep, extending beyond funding decisions for any given project. When Lowell visits Ariel, he brings his children and grandchildren, inspiring continuity, and intergenerational commitment. Similarly, the Lowell Milken Family Foundation selects clearly defined causes and objectives for support. And this past year, the Foundation sponsored Ariel educators to attend the National Institute of Excellence in Teaching (NIET), promoting collaboration across different philanthropic domains. By aligning clear goals and objectives with defined causes and needs, Lowell successfully creates a ripple effect of diverse and layered impact.

Of course, strategic impact doesn't require the capacity of a formidable family foundation. Nor does it require vast resources or non-stop philanthropic activity. It signifies a paradigm shift in philanthropy, a conscious move from spontaneous or reactionary giving to a more systematic and thoughtful approach. This change redefines not just the scope and size of your giving, but also the underlying methodology.

Will you examine whether your next gift is in line with your values and purpose before contributing? Will you think not only of the cause but of the giving chain and impact agents, if not for onetime donations, then for recurring gifts? Will you pursue the results of your giving, using impact outcomes to better inform your upcoming gifts? If the answer to all of these is yes, then both you, the funder, and the beneficiaries you support will benefit from your strategic approach to better giving.

If you're already practicing strategic philanthropy, you might want to skip to the next chapter to further refine your approach by designing a Kosher Giving Plan. However, if you're yet to systematically define your giving, consider starting with three preliminary stages to better prepare yourself: reflection, intention, and commitment.

Reflection

On the path to strategic giving, reflection involves looking back at your giving history with a critical eye. Consider moments when your giving felt most meaningful. What were the causes? How did they align with your values? Conversely, think about times when your giving felt less impactful or disconnected from your personal beliefs. Challenge yourself: can you be a better giver?

As we begin to reflect, we realize just how central giving is to who we are. We see that we are only scratching the surface of meaningful giving. Understanding what has been most meaningful and effective in your giving, you can identify what truly drives you to contribute. This awareness can lead to a heightened sense of purpose and a desire to maximize the impact of your philanthropic efforts. Recognizing the areas where you can make a real difference, and the values that are important to you, serves as a strong foundation for a more focused and strategic approach to giving.

Intention

Being intentional about your giving shifts your philanthropy from a conceptual strategy to one of active implementation. Imagine you've always felt passionate about education but have given sporadically to various educational causes without a clear focus. Adopting an intentional stance could mean focusing your efforts on a particular educational area, such as enhancing technological resources in underprivileged schools. This shift takes your strategy from a general inclination to a specific, targeted approach. Intentionality in giving ensures that each contribution you make is a conscious step in executing your strategic plan, rather than merely a response to a circumstantial request.

Intentionality in giving drives to the heart of mindful giving, not only in terms of the impact agents discussed earlier, but across the entire giving experience. Intentionality includes careful selection of causes, goal-oriented giving, and continuous commitment to projects of central significance.

Intentional giving also goes beyond financial contributions; it involves deciding your level of personal involvement in causes and projects, whether it's volunteering, advocacy, or serving on organizational boards.

Embracing an intentional mindset moves us closer to committed strategic philanthropy. When you're intentional about where, how, and why you give, it prompts you to think about the wider impact of your philanthropic efforts. This transition from impromptu or reactionary giving to a more deliberate approach encourages a deeper engagement with your philanthropic objectives.

Commitment to Strategy

I am honored to call General Charles C. Krulak, the 31st Commandant of the United States Marine Corps, my friend. At the age of 81, General Krulak is as sharp, focused, and relentless as ever. If there's one theme that recurs in virtually all our conversations, it's his passion for strategy. If it's something worth doing, it's worth doing it strategically.

Committing to strategic philanthropy requires a more significant investment than committing financial resources alone. It requires dedication to your chosen causes, engagement with the projects you support, and a willingness to learn and adapt. It also means staying informed about the impact your contributions make and remaining proactive about your philanthropy. This, to transform your reflection and intention into a thoughtful work process that leads to a meaningful personal journey.

The rewards of such a commitment to strategic giving are significant. It brings the deep satisfaction of knowing your contributions are truly making an impact. You gain personal growth as you deepen your understanding of the issues and communities you are passionate about. This strategic approach can lead to more effective philanthropy, where your resources are used in the most impactful way, aligning closely with your values and vision. Your commitment to strategic giving is, in essence, a commitment to your life's purpose and the causes you support.

On and off the battlefield, doing things well means doing them strategically. This principle of strategic action applies universally, even beyond the philanthropic arena. General Krulak doesn't have to be in the room for me to hear him enunciate the word 'stra-te-gic'.

Just as Maimonides added depth to the principles of kosher giving by providing pragmatic perspectives, a strategic outlook drives us to a comprehensive giving approach above and beyond casual philanthropy. It's a paradigm shift that begins with reflection, transitions to intention, and culminates with commitment.

Your Kosher Giving Plan will require your full engagement. Regardless of how much you're giving or to how many causes, strategic giving will allow you to best realize your purpose and your impact. It's about being faithful to your values and to the people you intend to support. Or, in the words of General Krulak and generations of US Marines, *Semper Fidelis*.

Kosher Food for Thought

How do you envision your giving commitments? Think about a cause you are passionate about. How could a more strategic approach to giving enhance your impact on this cause?

What challenges remain? When considering the shift to strategic giving, what are your main reservations or concerns?

Where does your purpose fit in? Imagine the potential outcomes of your strategic giving plan. How would realizing these outcomes help you realize your life's purpose?

Kosher Giving Applied Actions

1. Use your Kosher Giving Journal to record your answers to the Kosher Food for Thought above.

2. Define your commitment. Determine when you will begin developing your Kosher Giving Plan by designating a concrete date, schedule weekly sessions with yourself and/or your philanthropy partner and let those closest to you know that you will be embarking on a new, fresh giving journey.

3. Download the Kosher Giving Plan Workbook. Designate a time frame for the range of dates that your Kosher Giving Plan will prepare you for in the appropriate fields. There you have it. It's now in black on white. You're ready to begin.

Part 3: Your 4-Step Plan

Chapter Eight

Step 1: Design and Align Your Kosher Giving Plan

We've tackled the principles of kosher giving, defined the pillars and enhanced our appreciation for the forthcoming process with thoughtful perspectives. Now we commence with the how-to build and execute your Kosher Giving Plan.

Your Kosher Giving Plan will unfold in four steps: design, implementation, evaluation, and refinement. Each step plays a critical role in shaping a comprehensive and effective strategy. This chapter will focus on the first step: design. In this phase, you'll lay the groundwork for your giving, aligning your personal insights, goals, and aspirations with the causes that you support and the impact agents whom you work with.

The design step of your giving plan involves five factors: defining purpose, financial planning, needs identification, setting goals, and selecting impact agents. You'll note that in addition to our 3 pillars of purpose, impact agents and needs, it's important to include financial planning and goal setting in this process. Our focus is not to rehash what we discussed in Part 1, rather to provide the full range formula for your Kosher Giving Plan. The additional factors of finances and goals provide critical form and direction to this process.

It's important to note that while these five elements comprise the design step of your Kosher Giving Plan, the interaction between and among them is highly dynamic. Keep in mind that these are not consecutive phases that necessarily follow one another. As we discussed in our exploration of the principles and pillars of kosher giving, purpose, impact agents and needs are interactive. Our focus is not on which element we begin with, but rather on the inclusion of each and the alignment between them.

This chapter includes do-it-yourself procedures to tackle your Kosher Giving Plan head-on. Whatever order you choose to address the different elements, make sure to keep your Kosher Giving Journal and Giving Plan workbook close by so that you don't miss a beat. So long as you are careful to include each of these ingredients in your Kosher Giving Plan, you will be able to design a strategic plan with the potential for optimal impact.

Define Your Purpose

In Chapter 5, we began our exploration of personal and organizational purpose by considering our values and our roles. Here, as we design our Kosher Giving Plan, we're going to focus on the values that drive us and the interests that draw us. As we'll discover, our values and interests can and will be listed clearly so that we can align them with the other factors of our plan.

What matters to you? What are the issues or causes that you truly care about and consider important enough to support?

Before diving into the methodologies and guidelines for assessing your personal values and interests, take a moment to consider what truly matters to you. Think about the causes that spark your passion and compel you to action. Ask yourself what you genuinely care about and what you are ready and willing to support. This introspection is key to identifying the areas where your philanthropic efforts will not only be impactful but also deeply meaningful to you.

Remember, introspection often benefits from external perspectives. That looking inward often involves seeking the help of others. Engaging with mentors, advisors, or participating in group workshops can provide new perspectives and insights into your values and how they translate into actionable giving. These external inputs can be significant, acting as mirrors to your values, aiding you in shaping meaningful philanthropic actions.

Discover Your Philanthropic Foundation

So, take out your pen and paper, iPad, laptop, smartphone, or chisel and hammer, and let's begin the discovery of your values and interests. Whether you prefer a brainstorm or an organized list, the key is in the honesty and depth of your exploration. This is your opportunity to outline what drives you, forming the foundation for a unique philanthropic plan.

Start by listing apparent values like kindness or integrity. Then, move on to identifying your interests, whether broad like education or specific like environmental conservation. Remember, there's no right or wrong here—it's about what resonates with you on a personal level.

Taking a closer look means challenging yourself to uncover the values that lie beneath the surface. This involves digging deeper and questioning and exploring each value and interest you listed.

Ask yourself why each one matters to you and how it connects to your life experiences. This process might reveal more nuanced or complex values that weren't immediately apparent. The more you peel back the layers, the more you will discover the core principles that truly define and motivate you, providing a richer, more detailed foundation for your philanthropic plan.

Also, keep in mind that reflecting on difficult experiences is equally important in pinpointing your core values. Think about times that left you feeling uneasy or agitated. What occurred in these moments, and why were they so impactful to you? Often, these experiences are significant because they challenge values you hold dear. Understanding what values were tested or violated in these moments can provide profound insights into your fundamental principles. This reflection helps to paint a complete picture of your values, encompassing both the positive and the challenging aspects of your experiences.

Here are some specific guidelines to assist you in identifying your values and interests:

Self-Reflection through Journaling

Dedicate time to write about experiences that have shaped you, moments when you've felt most fulfilled, and causes that stir your passion to help uncover patterns in your interests and values.

Legacy Thinking

Think about the legacy you want to leave behind. Ask yourself how you want to be remembered and what impact you wish to make on the world. This can guide you towards causes that align with your long-term vision.

Consulting

If possible, work with a professional who can help you navigate this process. They can offer insights and methodologies tailored to your specific situation. This is something we, at Sector4, provide to our clients and giving partners. If you are looking for additional support as you work on your Kosher Giving Plan, reach out to us directly at info@Sector4.xyz.

Speak with Family and Friends

Sometimes, those close to us can provide valuable insights into our values and interests. Have open conversations about what they consider your passions and strengths.

Volunteer Experiences

Get involved in various social initiatives. Volunteering can provide hands-on experience with different causes and issues.

Review and Adapt

Recognize that your values and interests may evolve over time. Regularly revisit and revise your assessment to ensure its continued relevance.

Know that this is not a task to be completed in one sitting, but a gradual process of discovery. Allow yourself the space and patience to delve into these reflections, understanding that true self-awareness and clarity come with time. This journey of understanding your values and interests is as important as the philanthropic actions it will inform.

Prioritize

Once you have compiled a list of your values, ideally consisting of anywhere between 3 and 10, you face the next critical phase: prioritizing them. This process involves ranking these values in order of importance to you. Prioritizing helps to clarify which values are most central to your identity and philanthropic vision.

When prioritizing, you don't need a rigid scoring system, but understanding which values are most central to you is critical. Whether you choose to concentrate on a few core values or encompass a broader spectrum, the aim is to ensure your giving reflects what matters most to you. If addressing "the most pressing needs" is a core value, give it a specific focus, like "Iron Swords War Relief" or "local community support". While a general approach offers flexibility, defining your values with specificity enables more intentional planning and impactful philanthropy. As we later explore needs assessment, remember that clarity in your values leads to targeted and effective philanthropic strategies.

Record

Now it's time to record your findings. By the end of this introspective process, you should have a shortlist of values and interests - these are your central values. We've mentioned the Kosher Giving Plan Workbook (which can be downloaded at KosherGiving.com/tools), designed to accompany you as you develop your giving plan. I would suggest giving it a try, making sure to list your values in the designated fields. Be sure to include brief descriptions that add context. This will make your plan more meaningful and tailored to your unique perspective.

Financial Planning

Moving on to the second step, financial planning requires aligning your values with your financial resources. It's essential to reflect your values through numbers. This step involves translating the values and interests you've identified into a concrete financial plan. The goal is to ensure your financial contributions accurately mirror your core values, confirming that your investments genuinely represent what's most important to you. Effective financial planning is crucial not only for establishing a philanthropic budget but also for maintaining sustainable and impactful giving over time.

This process is thoughtful, diligent, and entirely achievable. While you may choose to consult a trusted financial advisor for guidance, it's beneficial to understand the various aspects involved in this process yourself. Familiarizing yourself with the nuances of financial planning will empower you to make informed decisions that reflect your philanthropic intentions and goals.

Budget

When determining your total giving budget, consider these financial parameters:

Your Finances

In determining your total giving budget, consider your commitment to philanthropy in relation to other forms of investment. Just as you would allocate resources to in relation to your financial portfolio, consider how much you would like to invest in social impact through your giving. This is strategic philanthropy, uplifting your giving from a casual expense to a predetermined investment.

Historical Giving Patterns

Examine your past donations to discern your typical giving trends and capacities. This analysis offers a practical foundation, helping you to understand what has been manageable and where there may be potential to increase your contributions. Utilizing this historical data ensures that your future giving plan is not only grounded in reality but also poised for greater impact, aligning with your financial capabilities and philanthropic aspirations.

Take the time to do your research. Pull out your financial statements, donation receipts, and records of past contributions. Record the budgets for your past three years of giving on our Kosher Giving Plan Excel file and categorize them according to your values and interests. This will help inform the coming year's budget and allocations.

Future Financial Goals

Balance your giving with other long-term objectives like retirement planning, education funds, and any potential significant purchases, integrating your philanthropy into your overall financial roadmap. This approach ensures that your charitable activities complement, rather than conflict with, your broader financial aspirations.

Your financial allocations in philanthropy are a tangible expression of your values. The process of balancing your philanthropic commitments with other life priorities is essential. You have the choice to prioritize philanthropy over other financial ventures, or the reverse. Approach this decision with honesty. The most effective and gratifying giving plans are those that resonate with your personal values and realistically fit within your financial means.

Potential Increase in Giving

When assessing the possibility of increasing your philanthropic contributions, it's vital to reflect on your current financial situation and your past giving patterns. Evaluate if you're in a position to give more than before, considering aspects like a rise in income, financial stability, or a desire to make a greater impact.

Flexibility in your giving plan is crucial, especially in crisis situations. For instance, in the event of a conflict like the Hamas-Israel War, consider your potential response. What could you do? How much could you stretch your giving? This isn't about drastic measures like liquidating assets, but understanding the extra funds you could allocate in times of need. This consideration helps in planning for unforeseen circumstances, ensuring you're prepared to respond effectively when necessary.

Amount

Deciding on the specific amount to allocate for philanthropy is meaningful, at times eye opening, and often provides food for thought. This figure should be a concrete number or clear percentage of your income or assets that you're comfortable dedicating to charitable causes. It's important to choose an amount that feels meaningful and impactful to you, yet is sustainable within your overall financial plan.

After setting your initial giving amount, consider adding another number for potential growth in your philanthropic budget. In our workbook, the first budgeted amount is referred to as "Commitment": this is the baseline sum that you plan to allocate, irrespective of the circumstances. The second sum is the "Expansion" budget sum, which reflects your thoughts about how much you might contribute beyond the baseline commitment. This expansion foresight into the growth of your philanthropic contributions can align with your financial growth, ensuring that as your capacity to give increases, so does your actual giving.

Allocation

Now that you have established a budget, it's time to align it with your values and interests. Doing so ensures that your financial commitment is directed toward causes you firmly believe in. Reflect on the list of values you've identified as central and important to you and consider how each prospective financial allocation aligns with these values. The introspective work you've done earlier now becomes invaluable, directing your decisions on where to allocate funds for maximum impact. This step ensures that your contributions meaningfully support the causes you care about while also fulfilling your own philanthropic aspirations.

Keep in mind, we're still in the planning phase of our giving strategy. Now's the time to proactively decide how you want your allocations to be structured in the upcoming year, rather than reacting to events as they happen.

As you start formulating your allocation plan, here are some key considerations to guide you in this process:

Diversification

Diversification in philanthropy refers to spreading your donations across a variety of causes and organizations. This approach is similar to diversifying investments in a financial portfolio. The idea is to support multiple initiatives, thereby maximizing the reach and impact of your philanthropic efforts.

Diversifying your giving can involve contributing to different sectors such as education, health, environment, or the arts, and can include a mix of local, national, and international organizations. This strategy not only helps mitigate risks associated with focusing on a single cause, but also reflects a holistic approach to addressing various societal needs and interests.

Impact Assessment

This process helps you determine which causes and organizations are using your funds most effectively to create tangible, positive changes. When assessing impact, consider factors like the organization's track record, the scalability of their initiatives, and the measurable outcomes they've achieved.

This assessment can guide you in allocating your budget towards causes where your contribution can make a significant difference, ensuring that your giving is not just well-intentioned, but also results in meaningful and lasting impact.

Personal Connection

Integrating a personal connection into your giving plan involves dedicating a portion of your budget to causes that are especially meaningful to you. This could be a cause that has directly impacted your life or one that aligns closely with your core beliefs and experiences.

Allowing room for personal connection in your philanthropy ensures that your giving is not only strategic, but also deeply fulfilling. It adds a layer of emotional engagement to your philanthropic efforts, making your contributions more meaningful to you and your beneficiaries.

The Babylonian Talmud states that "*the poor of your town come first*" (Bava Metzia 71A). Another type of personal connection is driven not by what moves your heart but by what's within your personal reach, influence and, to a degree, responsibility. This is an opportunity to consider how you may be instrumental in supporting causes that are present within your community, even if they're hidden from the public eye.

Strategic Alignment

It's time to zoom out. Strategic alignment in your giving plan involves ensuring that your budget allocation is in harmony with your broader philanthropic goals and objectives. This means choosing causes and organizations that not only align with your values and interests but also contribute to the long-term impact you wish to achieve through your giving. In this way, alignment ensures that your philanthropic efforts are focused, coordinated, and effective at realizing your desired outcomes.

In finalizing your allocation strategy, consider grouping your allocations according to specific categories or themes that reflect your values and interests. Our Kosher Giving Plan Workbook allows you to do this with ease. This categorization can help you organize your giving in a coherent and focused manner. It also aids in tracking and assessing the impact of your contributions in each category, making your philanthropy more strategic and impactful.

And remember, your allocation strategy is dynamic and can evolve as your interests or the needs of the world change.

Frequency

When deciding on the frequency of your contributions, consider whether monthly, annual, or event-specific donations best suit your financial plan and the nature of the causes you support. Regular, scheduled donations offer steady support to organizations, while onetime or event-driven contributions may be ideal for urgent needs or specific projects. Weigh the impact and practicality of each option, selecting a frequency that harmonizes with your lifestyle, financial circumstances, and philanthropic objectives.

Similarly, establishing a schedule to track your giving is essential for maintaining control and flexibility in your philanthropic endeavors. Under normal circumstances, a quarterly review of your contributions is a sensible strategy, allowing for periodic evaluation and adjustments to your plan. In more dynamic situations, like crises or conflicts, consider more frequent reviews, possibly monthly or even more regularly. This vigilant tracking ensures your giving stays attuned to evolving needs, enabling timely strategy refinements for optimal impact.

Integration, Flexibility and Taxes

As we wrap up the second factor, it's important to consider other financial planning aspects that, while not exclusive to giving, are crucial to factor in. Whether you navigate these elements independently or with an advisor, integrating your philanthropic efforts with broader financial and estate planning is important. This includes considering contingencies and tax implications, ensuring that your philanthropy is both sustainable and tax efficient. Preparing for contingencies guarantees uninterrupted support for your chosen causes, even amidst personal financial shifts, while understanding tax implications can benefit your overall financial health.

Adopting this comprehensive approach aligns your philanthropy with your long-term goals, securing a lasting and meaningful impact that resonates with both your values and financial strategies.

Identify Causes and Needs

In Chapter 3, we explored different methods for assessing needs, which can assist in pinpointing suitable projects and programs for your philanthropy. This included direct engagement with communities to grasp their needs, collaborating with local groups for deeper insights, employing data analysis and surveys to identify key issues, seeking expert advice, and considering both immediate and long-term requirements. This factor is where your needs assessment lives within your Kosher Giving Plan. If you need a refresher, flip back to Chapter 3 to review how to go about identifying needs. By applying these methods, you can ensure that your philanthropic efforts effectively match your values with the real needs of the causes you support.

Note that in our Kosher Giving Plan Workbook, we distinguish between causes and needs. Causes are the issues that you intend to address, such as education, poverty, or war relief. Needs are more specific in nature, such as a lack of computers in a particular school, meals for a homeless shelter or security equipment for a community. Causes are often defined in relation to proactive values and interests planning, whereas needs require a more specific study of the opportunities at hand. Your Kosher Giving Plan may commence with causes at the beginning, only to include specific needs at a later date.

It's important to remember the need for flexibility, especially during crises or conflicts. Situations can change rapidly, leading to sudden shifts in community needs. Adapting your assessment approach and financial allocation allows for a more responsive and effective reaction to these changes. This might mean reallocating resources to more urgent causes or adjusting your strategy to support new, emergent needs that arise because of the crisis. Maintaining this flexibility ensures that your philanthropy remains relevant, timely, and impactful, even in the most challenging circumstances.

Set Strategic Goals and Objectives:

The fourth factor is about crystallizing your philanthropic vision into strategic goals and objectives. Here is where you distinguish your broader aspirations from the specific, targeted outcomes you wish to achieve, and define what success looks like in your philanthropic journey. Whether it's influencing a certain number of lives, fostering distinct changes within a community, or contributing to meaningful progress in a particular field, these objectives should be tangible, quantifiable, and in harmony with the passion and purpose behind your giving. This crucial step elevates your philanthropy from a mere idea to a purpose-driven, goal-focused pursui t.

Remember, this step encompasses more than just your values. It integrates your broader vision and mission with the tangible impact you aim to achieve through your philanthropy.

These strategic goals and objectives are a direct reflection of your personal purpose as a philanthropist, centering on matters close your heart, as well as how you want to effect a change in the world. Consider it your roadmap for making a meaningful difference, guided by the deep sense of purpose you've defined for your philanthropic journey.

Distinguishing between goals and objectives will contribute to a clear giving strategy.

Goals are broad, overarching aspirations that reflect your vision, like 'improving education in underserved communities.' Objectives, on the other hand, are specific, measurable steps to achieve these goals, such as 'funding 100 scholarships for underprivileged students in a specific region, within a year.' This distinction helps in creating a focused and actionable plan, ensuring that every contribution you make is a step towards achieving your larger philanthropic aspirations.

For instance, if one of your goals is to support community development, an objective might be to fund a specific community center's after-school program for a year. This distinction ensures that your overall philanthropic vision (goals) and your immediate actions (objectives) are in harmony, creating a cohesive and impactful giving strategy.

Selecting Impact Agents and Funding Vehicles:

The fifth design factor of your plan requires you to move beyond notional commitments by choosing the philanthropic vehicles and methods for delivering your contributions. This involves deciding how you will give, be it through direct donations, establishing a charitable trust, participating in a donor-advised fund, or other forms of philanthropy.

Your selection should align with your specific goals, objectives, and preferred level of involvement. This is so that you find the most effective and satisfying way to direct your resources towards the causes that resonate with you, ensuring that your giving is as impactful and fulfilling as possible.

A key consideration in selecting your philanthropic vehicles is determining how involved you wish to be in your giving. Do you prefer directly overseeing projects and having close relationships with the causes you support? Or are you more comfortable contributing funds while others manage the specifics? Your choice will guide you towards establishing a personal foundation, engaging in direct giving, or opting for a donor-advised fund, shaping the nature of your impact and your connection to your philanthropic activities.

Choose Your Giving Vehicles

There is no shortage of options when it comes to the various ways to give. A complete Kosher Giving Plan requires you to choose not only how much you're giving and where you're giving, but the infrastructure that you will use to make your allocations.

- Direct donations: Giving directly to charities or causes.
- Charitable trusts or foundations: Creating or contributing to a foundation for more structured giving.
- Donor-advised funds: Contributing to a fund that allows you to recommend grants to charities.
- Volunteering or in-kind contributions: Offering your time or non-monetary resources.
- Impact investing: Investing in ventures that generate social or environmental impact, in addition to financial returns.

As you consider your philanthropy options, remember the impact agency choices from Chapter 4. We explored roles of non-profits, NGOs, and social enterprises for varying levels of direct project involvement and impact investments. Our coverage also included volunteer coordinators for hands-on support, research teams for data-driven giving, and foundations for long-term commitments, along with governmental and CSR entities for policy alignment. Each option, including accessible online and crowdfunding platforms, offers a distinct approach to executing your giving strategy, tailored to fulfill your specific philanthropic goals and objectives.

Consider Consulting

You're committed to philanthropy, but navigating the wide range of options can be daunting, especially when it's not your day job. This is where a trusted advisor becomes invaluable, offering clarity and guidance to streamline your giving plan and make the process manageable and effective.

Strategic advisors bring in-depth knowledge of the philanthropic landscape and can guide you towards options that best suit your goals and style of giving. At Sector4 Strategy, we help you navigate the complexities of various philanthropic vehicles, ensure alignment with your values, and optimize the impact of your contributions. Utilizing our expertise or that of other consultants can be invaluable in making informed decisions, ensuring your philanthropy is both effective and fulfilling.

Your First Milestone

You've done it! You've committed and you've executed. It took you time, patience, effort, and dedication, but you've reached your first milestone. By filling out each of the fields in your Giving Plan Workbook, you've created your blueprint for giving.

This file includes each of the five factors in an organized structure that will allow you to follow through with implementation, evaluation, and refinement. It's the asset that will guide your giving going forward, and it's one of the most meaningful gifts that you can give to yourself and your philanthropic partners.

Now that you've created your dynamic giving plan, take a moment to appreciate the significant progress you've made on your philanthropic journey. As we move forward to implement your plan, remember the importance of what you've accomplished. Celebrate this milestone; it signifies a profound commitment to positive change and marks a pivotal moment in your journey of giving.

Kosher Food for Thought

Reflect on your assessment of personal values and interests. How did exploring your values and interests reshape your understanding of what you wish to achieve through philanthropy?

Are you more confident in your financial planning skills? Regarding your financial commitment to philanthropy, which insights have you gained about balancing your personal goals with your desire to give?

How has the process of researching and identifying causes deepened your connection to the issues you care about? How did choosing specific philanthropic vehicles and methods resonate with your personal approach to making an impact?

Do you feel more knowledgeable about your strategic giving process? What did the process of setting strategic goals and objectives reveal about your aspirations and priorities in giving?

Kosher Giving Applied Actions

1. Use your Kosher Giving Journal to record your answers to the Kosher Food for Thought above.

2. If you haven't yet done so, download the Kosher Giving Plan Workbook.

3. The Workbook has designated spaces for each of the tasks that appear in this chapter. Review, respond and record carefully. This is your Plan. Diligence will lead to outcomes.

Chapter Nine

Step 2: Implementation

Bruce Johnston, a resident of Birmingham Alabama, had been running a values-driven life-experience facility in northern California for years. JH Ranch caters to Christian teens, adults and families who have heard about the content-rich and exhilarating programming that the outdoor training site offers. The program had built a strong reputation and was on a growth path when Bruce accepted an invitation to meet the then-Mayor of Ariel, Ron Nachman.

During a visit to the city, Bruce and Ron got along famously. The two visionaries discussed and started to plan a partnership through which an outdoor leadership development training facility would be established in Ariel. But Bruce's new commitment was not without its drawbacks. After sharing his vision for supporting the project in Ariel to the ranch's leading donors, they got into their cars, drove off the property, and left Bruce with nothing more than a fresh start. The finances weren't there, but the commitment was unwavering.

As Bruce tended to the ranch, his wife, Heather, took the lead on the Israel project. What began as a lone alpine tower became the largest outdoor training center in Israel. The Ariel National Leadership Development Center, or National Leadership Center (NLC), is presently an informal education center that has trained over 100,000 participants. With new ropes courses and training facilities added from year to year, NLC continues to enlist new funders, leaders, trainers and visiting groups. But the cultivation of the resources has never been the primary focus of the operation. The focus has always been educational content.

Heather aimed to translate 30 years' worth of biblically inspired leadership content into the NLC curriculum. It seemed like a perfect fit, considering Israel's status as the Jewish State. But this was more challenging than originally expected. "Bible" doesn't mean the same thing for Jews as it means for Christians. It wasn't enough to translate the content from English to Hebrew, or to adorn brochures with Stars of David. It necessitated an in-depth analysis and thorough adaptation of the content to cater to visitors from across Israel and occasionally from abroad.

The strength of Heather and Bruce's vision persevered. The content was carefully adjusted to accommodate the audience. This fine-tooth review and refinement process required a heightened inter-cultural appreciation and a deep respect. Heather was undeterred, committed to trusted relationships with her partners in Ariel and throughout Israel's Ministry of Education, and she educates her friends and supporters accordingly.

Whenever we hit bumps along the road, Heather swiftly and decisively tended to them. This has always been the case, whether a volunteer wasn't sufficiently careful about Jewish faith sensitivities, or a partnering organization wasn't pulling its weight. For nearly 15 years, Heather has seen to it that the NLC is a place of excellence.

Her work with the Ministry of Education has been extensive and consistent. In addition to coordinating the content, Heather's relationships have paved the path for many groups to visit. Recognized as an approved site with groups partially funded by the Ministry of Education, the NLC has evolved into an accurate embodiment of its founders' original vision.

NLC's upcoming 15-year anniversary is an opportunity to consider the kind of commitment, grit, and innovative thinking required to implement the ambitious undertaking of establishing and operating a national informal education facility. Notwithstanding the bumps along the road, the commitment to vision has meant a commitment to implementation.

As we embark on Step Two of our Kosher Giving Plan, we shift gears from planning to implementation. This phase is about bringing your carefully crafted strategy to life. It's where your ideas, values, and financial commitments are transformed into meaningful actions. Implementing your plan effectively requires diligence, coordination, and sometimes a degree of flexibility to adapt to changing circumstances. It's a significant transition from planning to actual impact, marking another milestone in your kosher giving journey.

Initiate Your Strategic Plan

Initiating your giving plan involves turning the strategic blueprint of your Kosher Giving Plan into reality. This crucial step involves engaging with the organizations or initiatives you've selected, starting your financial contributions as per your schedule, and starting any hands-on involvement you've planned, such as volunteering or board participation.

This step bridges the divide between conceptual planning and practical execution, bringing your intentions and well-crafted plans to life in the areas and causes you're passionate about. Remember, this initial step sets the tone for the overall execution of your Kosher Giving Plan. To get started, make sure to use do the following:

Communicate

Reach out to the organizations or causes you've chosen to support. Establish clear communication channels, understand their requirements and how you can best support their needs.

Complete Your Financial Setup

Set up the necessary financial mechanisms for your contributions, whether it's through bank transfers, setting up a fund, or other means.

Schedule the Implementation

Start making contributions according to the schedule you've outlined in your plan, regardless of whether they're onetime donations, recurring contributions, or timed to specific events or needs.

Actively Engage with Your Causes

If your plan includes personal involvement, like volunteering, start participating in these activities.

Document the Process

Keep records of your activities and contributions for future reference and assessment. You'll need this for your Kosher Giving Plan file, as well as for the following phases of evaluation and refinement.

Adapt to Evolving Needs

In philanthropy, adapting allows you to respond effectively to changing circumstances and evolving needs. It involves being open to reassessing and modifying your approach, based on new information, unexpected challenges, or shifts in the areas you support. This adaptability ensures your philanthropic efforts remain relevant, impactful, and aligned with your goals; even as external conditions fluctuate.

Embracing a flexible mindset also enables you to navigate unforeseen situations, such as changes in the socio-political landscape, shifts in community needs, or even global events like the Iron Swords War, without losing sight of your philanthropic vision.

We met Shmil Atlas of Israel Heart2Heart in Chapter 5. When he accommodates an influx of equipment; he is adapting. When he pivots back to Israel Heart2Heart's core mission, he is adapting again. These effective pivots may seem intuitive, but they are oftentimes the exception to the rule and not the rule itself.

> **Successful adaptation requires a mix of skill, experience, and clarity of vision.**

Here are some techniques to take into consideration:

Stay Informed

Regularly update yourself on the current situation and needs of the causes you support. This could involve reading reports, communicating with organizations, or staying tuned to relevant news.

Seek Feedback

Make sure to check in with the organizations or individuals you support. They can provide valuable insights into what is working and what needs adjustment.

Evaluate Impact

Continuously assess the impact of your contributions. Are they meeting the goals you set? If not, it may be time to rethink your Kosher Giving Plan.

Be Willing to Change Course

If a particular approach or partnership isn't yielding the desired results, or if new, more pressing needs emerge, don't hesitate to reallocate resources or shift focus. This can be difficult at first, but it's intended to be more effective going forward.

Identify Major Changes:

Sometimes an adaptation is not enough. If major changes are needed, consider consulting with your philanthropic advisor to ensure that any changes align with your overall goals and values.

Actively Engage & Participate in Giving

Engaging with your philanthropic partners is another part of the implementation phase. This involves building relationships with the organizations or causes you support, understanding their work on a deeper level, and actively participating in their missions. Engagement can take various forms, from regular communication and site visits to participating in decision-making processes or volunteering, allowing for a more immersive and meaningful giving experience.

Direct engagement in philanthropy is demanding, but it's also a win-win. For donors, it provides a deeper sense of fulfillment and a clearer understanding of the impact of contributions. It allows for more meaningful interactions and stronger relationships with impact agents, fostering trust and collaboration. This closer involvement often also leads to better informed decisions, as the recipients can also access your valuable insights and expertise. Ultimately, this enhances the overall effectiveness and sustainability of your Kosher Giving Plan and your impact.

You don't have to commit yourself to a 15-year implementation process like Heather Johnston did or hop on a plane (or series of flights) from Alabama to Israel to address pressing developments and solve issues as they arise. Your Kosher Giving Plan's implementation, coupled with your direct engagement and adaptability, should correspond to the degree that you've committed yourself to any given project.

After all, implementation need not be limited to sending a donation in the mail. Know that for those special projects, the ones closest to your heart, there's so much more that you can do.

Kosher Food for Thought

What insights surfaced as you began putting your giving plan into action? How has this been a learning experience for you?

What does adaptation in philanthropy mean to you? As you record your giving journey, make notes of situations where you had to adapt your giving strategy during implementation. How comfortable are you being flexible with your giving?

Which cause or project draws you to engage directly? How has that engagement affected you? How has it affected your impact?

Kosher Giving Applied Actions

1. Use your Kosher Giving Journal to record your answers to the Kosher Food for Thought above.

2. Use your Kosher Giving Plan Workbook to track your plan's implementation.

3. Define parameters. Record what constitutes a change in course that warrants a fresh review of your giving to a specific cause.

4. Define engagement. Indicate how you will be involved in the causes you care most about. Include references to your primary points of contact.

Chapter Ten

Step 3: Measure and Evaluate

Having initiated your Kosher Giving Plan, you are now seeing your resources meaningfully invested in projects that resonate with your values and interests. The active role you've taken with your most cherished organizations amplifies the sense of purpose in your life. However, there's one question that persists: are these efforts truly making a difference?

Step 3 of your Kosher Giving Plan focuses on measuring and evaluating the impact. We assess 'impact' to ensure our resources are effectively utilized and to meet our beneficiaries' expectations. This evaluation also informs and enhances our future philanthropy.

Effective philanthropy is rooted in accountability and continuous improvement. Your philanthropic journey is an ongoing process, and understanding your impact is a necessary step to ensuring your efforts are as meaningful and effective as possible.

In some ways, complex situations like the Iron Swords War make measuring impact more challenging, as highly dynamic environments require a flexible approach to evaluation. And yet, in other ways, the rush to deliver urgent aid can yield clear indicators of success or a lack thereof. For example, tracking whether bulletproof vests reached their intended recipients offers a straightforward measure of success, despite the complexity of the implementation process.

As you integrate measurement tools into your Kosher Giving Plan, here are five fundamental guidelines to direct your approach:

1: Define Metrics

What are your benchmarks? Defining clear metrics is a first step in the impact measurement process. This involves identifying specific, quantifiable indicators that align closely with your objectives.

Start by asking what success looks like for each of your goals. For example, if your aim is to improve education, relevant metrics could include literacy rates, graduation rates, or student engagement levels.

It's important to ensure these metrics are not only relevant, but realistically measurable. Consider both quantitative data, like numbers and percentages, and qualitative data, like personal stories and testimonials, which can provide deeper insights into the impact of your giving. Well-defined metrics are the foundation of effective impact analysis.

2: Collect Data

Collecting data is the next step. This involves gathering information that corresponds to your defined metrics. Depending on your goals, data collection can vary from simple counts like the number of people served by a program, to more complex methods like conducting surveys, interviews, or focus groups.

Partnering with the organizations you fund can provide valuable data, as they often have direct access to this information. Also, consider leveraging technology for efficient data collection. Regular and consistent data collection is helpful, as it allows for tracking progress over time and makes your impact assessment more robust and reliable. Remember, the quality and relevance of the data collected are critical for an accurate understanding of your philanthropic impact.

Five weeks into the Iron Swords War, the Jewish Federations of North America had collectively raised $657,395,394 as indicated in their 38-page November 16, 2023 Israel Emergency Fund Allocations Update. Of the funds raised, $187,970,845 had already been allocated. The consistent reports were transparent in terms of programs, recipients, and decision-making policy. They also included descriptions of each of the beneficiary organizations, alphabetized, of course. The data collection was impressive, and the presentation was easy to understand.

Accurate data is another step in the evaluation process, but allocations alone don't tell the story of how the funds were expended. That requires us to dig deeper.

3: Receive Feedback

Ideally, we want feedback directly from beneficiaries. This can be achieved through personal conversations, by conducting surveys or structured interviews, facilitating open forums for discussion, and offering anonymous feedback channels online or through suggestion boxes.

You'll need to be actively listening, ensuring that beneficiaries feel comfortable and valued in sharing their experiences. Direct feedback provides a clear window into the actual impact of your philanthropy, allowing you to fine-tune your approach to better meet the needs of those you aim to help.

But there are times when it's not appropriate or even possible to engage directly with beneficiaries. In these cases, working closely with your impact agents—the organizations and intermediaries that help facilitate your philanthropy—becomes invaluable. They can provide detailed reports, insights, and analyses that are critical for understanding the impact of your contributions.

These organizations often have direct contact with beneficiaries and can relay feedback, concerns, and successes. Collaborating with them enhances the accuracy of your impact assessment and ensures your philanthropic efforts are aligned with the actual needs and circumstances of those you're aiming to help.

It's worth noting that some impact agents are uncomfortable with impact assessments. When it comes to nonprofits, for example, they are committed to their work; they are often under-funded, and they can personally attest to the impact of their efforts. They may feel undermined, second-guessed, or unappreciated when questioned about the degree to which their work yields measurable results.

It's helpful, and at times necessary, to communicate to your impact agents that you are not testing them, but rather encouraging them. You share the same goals and objectives, you've all committed valuable resources of time, talent, and treasure, and you all want to see maximum results from your valuable investment. It's shared value, and it benefits everyone who's engaged in the giving process.

Thoughtful impact assessment can help an organization's leadership move from doing good to realizing results. It makes accountability and transparency an industry standard. And it can generate efficiencies and innovative focus when adaptation and flexibility matter the most.

4: Assess Efficiency

The first daily cause featured on KosherGiving.com was a story about Gal Barzilay. Gal, who had served as an Israel Defense Forces officer along the Gaza border during her active-duty military career, is the Chief Operating Officer of Boosst, a Tel Aviv based software company. As the CEO of Boosst was called for reserve duty, Gal found herself wearing two new hats: stepping in to steer her company towards continued growth and applying her skills to serve a nation reeling from devastation.

Gal is one of the founders of Hitech4israel. It was one week into the war when we spoke: "Hitech4israel was born on the second day of the war with 25 industry leaders at the first meeting. Now, we have grown to 250 volunteers, with 50 dedicating significant time daily," The group of tech professionals organized swiftly from across the industry. They knew that their skills set could prove critical in bringing focus and results to an otherwise numb and disjointed environment.

The issue of over 200 Israelis, mostly civilians, weighed heavily on Israel in general and on the members of Hitech4israel in particular. Some of them had survived the massacre of outdoor party goers, others had friends who were kidnapped or murdered on October 7. Their response was practical and effective. "Addressing the challenge of locating each individual, especially without direct access to Gaza and the clutter of social media, is immense. But Hitech4israel is making strides. We've been diligently sifting through online data, extracting vital information, and collaborating with security forces to make sense of the chaos and work towards bringing our people home."

Parallel to their close coordination with security forces, they developed efficiencies where other well intentioned social entrepreneurs fell short. "The massive draft of reserve forces across Israel revealed a need for additional supplies. The Hitech4israel organization quickly found solutions to identify the needs of 200 regular service, reserve duty, and first response units. Thirteen units have already benefited from our efforts in raising funds, marshaling volunteers, and coordinating logistics," Gal explained.

Metrics. Data. Impact. Efficiency.

Gal also added an important insight, typical of the Israeli tech industry, and critical for everyone at this time. "We're here to fill a void. I'm driven by firm belief and by the courage to fail, to learn, and to make things better."

To fail, to learn, and to make things better. Words spoken by a young lady in her twenties of uncompromising fortitude. Words that can enlighten a nation and guide a generation.

Efficiency doesn't mean perfection. Impact measurement doesn't mean unrealistic expectations. We measure so that we can learn both from successes and from failures. If something doesn't go right with your Kosher Giving Plan, that doesn't mean that it can't be fixed. Your commitment to your values and goals is steadfast. Your efforts are on target. And your plan is dynamic, designed for adaptation and improvement.

5: Be Adaptable in Focus

I had long been aware of Leket's work as Israel's leading food bank, but I hadn't taken interest in their operations until speaking with Rechelle Hochhauser, who had recently been recruited to their staff. "Everything is tech. It's highly efficient and really impressive". Coming from Rechelle, an accomplished and high performing nonprofit professional in her own right, this was saying a lot.

Joseph Gitler, Leket's Founder and Chairperson, moved with his wife and children from New York to Israel in September 2000.

Their timing was a bit awkward. The Second Palestinian Intifada, or uprising, had just begun. Bus bombings, shootings and all forms of violent terror were plaguing Israelis day in and day out. Joseph and his family were undeterred.

But there was something that bothered Joseph. He noticed that different Israelis were living through these trying experiences in very different ways from one another. There were those with means and those without. Both groups were experiencing stress and anxiety, but their points of departure were different, significantly impacting their ability to cope. He sensed a disconnect, and that drove him to action.

Joseph discovered countless organizations that were caring for the poor and distributing food. He also discovered that they were spending significant time and resources raising the funds necessary to purchase the food that they were preparing and distributing. Something didn't compute.

Joseph circled back to the disconnect. Everyone was under pressure, but some people had more than others. Why raise money for food when there's plenty of food to be found? Why make new meals for some people when other people are throwing so much quality food away? Why not match the resources with the needs?

The first step was to ask the nonprofits if they would distribute food that was gifted by caterers, hotels, and event halls. The answer was a resounding yes.

The second step was to turn on the charm and ask the caterers, hotels, and event halls if they would be willing to pass on their unused food items to feed the needy. This was a more difficult ask. It was commonplace to dispose of whatever was left over, and change isn't easily embraced. "I'm still convinced that it was my American accent that carried the day. It was disarming and innocent," Joseph explains. Phone call after phone call, meeting after meeting, everyone said yes.

Great ideas are a good starting point. Buy-in from stakeholders is a great next step. But then what?

"For the first month, I got into my Subaru and started picking up the food. If I got a call, I went. There were some mismatches at first when people said, 'I have a lot of leftovers' and that meant three chicken thighs, but we learned, and we grew more efficient". After all, efficiency is the name of the game.

At first, the growing efficiency and logistics operation was named Table to Table. The name conveyed a compelling image of caring for those in need by providing the same quality meals that would otherwise be served at the finest events and halls. But Table to Table doesn't translate very well to Hebrew, and as the organization grew it needed a new brand.

"Our organization is not religiously observant," Joseph continues, describing the genesis of how the new name came about. They serve everyone and they are led and staffed by Israelis of all walks of life. "But I did want a name that was connected to our heritage, to the State of Israel, to the land of Israel and to the Torah."

"*Leket* (literally gleaning) is the name of one of three basic forms of gifts left for the poor, as described in the Torah. This is exactly what we do."

Joseph is referring to Leviticus 19: 9-10 where 'leket' is described as the directive to leave some of your harvest for those who have less. If you drop small amounts of fruits and vegetables when you harvest, leave them alone. Don't gather them for yourself. Someone else needs them more than you do.

And so, Joseph and his team renamed their organization "Leket Israel". Their operation has since grown exponentially. Today they have 150 employees and an efficiency rate that gets tens of thousands of tons of food delivered to the needy for far less than cost. A little more than a dollar gets a healthy, safe, and nutritious meal rescued from waste, transported, and delivered to someone who values it more than we can imagine. Leket is now a household name in Israel, serving as one of the country's leading and most respected nonprofits.

But "the world changed for everyone, and for Leket, with the outbreak of the war", Joseph explains. Leket's bread and butter is the rescue of fruits and vegetables from farms and the rescue of cooked food from the army, hotels, and caterers. Now the army bases are essentially inaccessible. The hotel and catering hall events have dried up. The fruits and vegetables are barely harvested enough to meet the demands of the marketplace, as foreign workers have left the fields. Less food rescue means less for those in need.

On an October 7 Saturday night team call, Leket understood that this was going to be like Covid-19 on steroids. Leket would have to feed the poor not by saving meals but by buying them.

Leket got to work. With the help of the goodwill of the community and thanks to their strong reputation, they've been able to purchase and distribute 15,000 meals a day at a nominal cost. They've also begun purchasing dry goods, enough to prepare 60,000 packages, purchasing items from hard hit businesses whenever possible. During month one of the war, they spent 5 million dollars to meet these demands.

Due to their extensive relationships with Israel's farms, Leket stepped in to fill another wartime need. Instead of rescuing farm surpluses for the needy, they've been assisting those same farmers to make ends meet.

Over the past few weeks, Leket has placed over 25,000 volunteers at Israeli farms, mostly in the southern border communities. These volunteers include Israelis and visitors from overseas. What began as individuals has grown to entire groups, soon to include 800 university students with tuition scholarships from Bank Leumi in recognition of the young adults' efforts on behalf of national priorities.

Leket is now, for the first time, buying food directly from the farmers to feed those in need. They normally rescue between 25,000 and 30,000 tons of crops per year, but now they're purchasing crops to support the farmers and provide for food security - a budget increase of 8 million dollars. These are temporary adaptations for an organization that is large enough to make a nationwide impact and innovative enough to address the most pressing needs.

Just like Gal Barzilay, Joseph feels the need to fill in the gaps: "The economic impact of this war in the short and long term has been catastrophic. Civil society has been incredible," he explains. "But at a certain point, the motivated individual runs out of money for donations or must return to work or school. When that happens, the well-established organizations need to step in and fill that void."

Effective impact measurement is a careful blend of quantitative and qualitative assessments that allows us to identify and fill gaps. Whatever tools you use to evaluate what you've accomplished, keep in mind that this assessment process begins with the initial design of your Kosher Giving Plan. When defining your values and aligning them with causes and needs, think not only about intentions but about results. How will your gifts make a difference? How will they lead change? And how will you measure success?

Metrics, data and feedback are the building blocks of our assessment. They pave a path towards efficiency, informing how we can give better during this giving season and how we can refine our Kosher Giving Plan in anticipation of the next giving season. Efficiency translates into a greater sense of purpose for the donor, better partnerships with impact agents, and better outcomes for the beneficiary.

Ultimately, our evaluation process leads us towards refinement, the fourth step of the Kosher Giving Plan. With experience-based information at our fingertips, a thoughtful learning process and the ability to adapt, the next season of giving can be even more rewarding than the last.

Kosher Food for Thought

Are you making the most of your metrics? Do the metrics you've chosen for measuring impact reflect your core values and philanthropic goals?

How do you approach beneficiary feedback? What can you do to improve your methods of obtaining direct feedback from beneficiaries to better understand the impact of your giving?

Reflect on your collaborations with impact agents. In what ways can you enhance collaboration with impact agents to improve outcomes?

Are you able to adapt to complex situations? How flexible is your approach to measuring impact, especially in complex situations like the Iron Swords War?

Kosher Giving Applied Actions

1. Use your Kosher Giving Journal to record your answers to the Kosher Food for Thought above.

2. Use your Kosher Giving Plan Workbook to track metrics in the designated fields.

3. Compare outcomes from one year to the next. If this is your first annual Kosher Giving Plan, compare outcomes to your expectations. If you're tracking results for a renewed Plan, compared to the outcomes from previous years.

Chapter Eleven

Step 4: Refine

We now arrive at the fourth step of our Kosher Giving Plan. This step draws from our experiences in the previous three steps to better inform what our plan will look like in the coming season or in the year ahead. While the previous chapter guided us through practical aspects of assessing the impact of our philanthropy, we now shift towards introspection and strategic recalibration.

This chapter centers on the ongoing process of enhancement and personal growth in philanthropy. It emphasizes the significance of applying insights gained from evaluating our impact to refine our strategies. This continual refinement ensures that our future giving is more attuned to our evolving understanding, values, and the dynamic landscape of needs. It's about adapting and growing, ensuring that our philanthropic efforts remain relevant and effective in an ever-changing landscape of needs.

Refinement, as the fourth step of the Kosher Giving Plan, represents a continuous process, rather than a final step. It's an upward spiral leading to constant improvement and advancement. Each iteration of refinement elevates your philanthropic efforts, ensuring they resonate more effectively with your evolving values and the shifting landscape of needs. It involves assessing what has been achieved, learning from triumphs and challenges, and applying these lessons to forge ahead more effectively. This ongoing process of refinement keeps your giving dynamic, relevant, and meaningful.

At its best, your Kosher Giving Plan will seamlessly integrate the refinement phase into its workflow. This integration allows for constant evolution and improvement, ensuring that the plan remains dynamic and responsive; a living strategy that adapts and grows over time. This continuous cycle of reflection, learning, and improvement is important for the execution of your current Kosher Giving Plan and will guide the adjustments that you incorporate into next year's updated version.

Drawing Conclusions

Post-measurement and assessment, refinement involves interpreting the gathered insights and applying them to your Kosher Giving Plan. The following processes are helpful in formulating conclusions:

Outcome Evaluation

Here, we analyze the data and feedback, understanding the implications of making informed decisions, and translating diverse interpretations into a unified strategy.

Strategy Adjustment

This is easier said than done, and significant changes in your Kosher Giving Plan should be approached with caution and may benefit from a second opinion, such as further team discussions or consulting a professional advisor.

Continuous Improvement

Your Kosher Giving Plan should be reviewed and renewed regularly. Bridging your previous year's work into the coming year, refinement is an ongoing process that can create efficiencies and needs adjustments on a rolling basis. Do not wait until your annual review, especially in times of crisis.

Personal Growth

Don't forget yourself in the process. The refinement phase should also focus on your growth as a kosher giving philanthropist, reflecting on your values, purpose, and goals. If you're growing, your Kosher Giving Plan is effective; if not, it may be time to refine your approach or objectives.

Application based on Conclusions

You've conducted thorough research and drawn insightful conclusions. Now, it's time to apply these understandings to your Kosher Giving Plan. Use the guidelines below to revisit the pillars of kosher giving, allowing you to reassess and refine your plan's various components. Utilize your Kosher Giving Plan to determine necessary changes and their extent.

1: Make Budget Adjustments

Does your initial budget need to be increased or decreased? Is it time to reallocate funds based on emerging needs or changes in your financial situation? Record your budget adjustments and make decisions about causes and project allocations accordingly.

2: Revisit Allocations

Reflect on the distribution of your resources. Are the causes and organizations you're supporting still aligned with your values and the objectives you set? Assessing your allocations regularly allows you to pivot toward areas that may now be more aligned with your evolving interests or emergent needs.

3: Adjust Your Frequency of Giving

It's worthwhile to reassess how often you contribute. Have your circumstances changed, allowing for more frequent giving, or do you need to space out your contributions? Adapting the frequency can help you maintain a consistent impact over time.

4: Check Your Engagement Levels

How involved are you with the causes you support? Do you desire deeper involvement, or do you need to take a step back? Remember, engagement isn't just about signing a cheque; your time, expertise, and personal connection to the cause are just as important.

5: Assess Feedback and Report

Are you receiving the kind of feedback and reports from your philanthropic investments that help you understand their impact? If not, it might be time to request more detailed information or change your approach to monitoring.

6: Evaluate Your Impact Agent Relationships

Consider the effectiveness of your interactions with impact agents. Are they providing the guidance and support you need? If your philanthropic goals have evolved, ensure your trusted team members are aligned with your current vision.

7: Check Operational Efficiencies

Assess the efficiency of how your philanthropy is managed. This could involve administrative aspects, the use of technology, collaborations with partners, or the vehicles through which you make your contributions.

8: Consider Your Responsiveness to Emergencies

Reflect on how your giving plan accommodates sudden crises or emergencies. The Iron Swords War, for example, might have shown the need for more flexible or rapid responses in your philanthropy. Have you been able to respond? Which parameters need to be adjusted for greater flexibility, in the short or long term?

9: Reflect on Your Legacy and Long-term Planning

Your Kosher Giving Plan is focused on your annual giving, but it includes your legacy goals, projects, and budgets as well. As you refine your plan, look ahead and think about the legacy you are building through your philanthropy. What changes do you need to make for your giving to align with the long-term impact you wish to have?

Each parameter in this refinement process is interconnected. Approach each step comprehensively, challenging yourself to improve continuously, and seizing every opportunity to forge a clearer, more impactful path forward.

Reconfiguration and Reflection on your Kosher Giving Plan

Andy Toles pulled the Integrated Business Roundtable together with the efficiency of a well-connected professional and the stealth of a quiet and unassuming purpose-driven steward. He had attended the first international Israeli-Palestinian Economic Forum in 2019, where I challenged attendees not only to applaud efforts to improve business ties between the two populations, but to invest in those businesses as well. Andy answered the call.

We converged at Mike Humphrey's Texas lake house for an intense, three-day discovery and planning session. For most of us, this was the first time we had met one another in person. We knew that we wanted to discern the potential for financial investment into inter-population startups and companies, but first we needed to better appreciate who our would-be partners might be. We played it by the book, discussing values, visions, missions, goals, and objectives.

Our discussion about values was intriguing, considering the participants' different backgrounds and perspectives. The common denominator was that everyone cared for Israel and everyone saw economic development as a positive force.

Jay Hein, CEO of the Sagamore Institute in Indianapolis, was well versed in economic impact initiatives, having launched the Minority Entrepreneurship Institute as one of numerous such programs in the United States and beyond. We were joined by Mike Humphrey, chairman of the Prisoners Entrepreneurship Program, Norm Schulz, a respected consultant, Mike O'Neil, a leading industrialist, and Andy Toles, an expert in law and global networks. Together, we compiled a set of skills and acumen that was far greater than the sum of its parts.

Navigating our diverse experiences and the array of viewpoints that surpassed our initial common ground, it became essential to explicitly express our core motivations. This process was key in deciding if, beyond the early ties of friendship, we were truly aligned in our desire to collaborate professionally. Understanding what drives each of us was crucial in determining the potential for a successful and harmonious working relationship.

I'll admit it - I did a lot of the talking. As the only Jew and Israeli in the room, and as the party responsible for casting the vision, it was on me to provide content to the structured discussions.

I made presentations about Israel, relationships between Israelis and Palestinians, the business-sphere, realistic expectations about what could and couldn't be accomplished, inter-cultural sensitivities (Jewish-Christian and Israeli-Palestinian), and the values that lay at the foundation of everything that was more editorial than factual. The team took it all in and arrived at a shared commitment to purpose.

We successfully balanced several key values: the significance of an Israeli presence in Judea and Samaria (the West Bank), the importance of proactive Israeli-Palestinian cooperation, the value of Christian engagement with the region, the respect for intercultural understanding, and the commitment to community-wide investment. By aligning these values, we created a foundation upon which we could develop and move forward with a cohesive action pl an.

Our regular team calls were followed by a two-day methodology development session in Washington, DC. We decided to take the impact investing route, activating philanthropic Donor Advised Funds for investments. What emerged was a hybrid giving-plan-business-plan. Some of our metrics were defined by the philanthropic capital that was invested, while other outcomes were to be measured by the growth of the beneficiary businesses. The plan was designed to run for three years, which is precisely what it did.

We launched the Integrated Business Roundtable on January 1, 2020, completely unaware that Covid-19 would soon change the world as we knew it. Challenging and unpredictable as that season was, we succeeded in meeting our goals and reaching our milestones.

We also launched a first-of-its kind Investment Showcase, where we successfully invested one million shekels of Donor Advised Funds into two start-ups that met our criteria. IBR also assumed the funding responsibility for the Israeli Palestinian Economic Forum, hosted online due to Covid-19 restrictions.

We subsequently initiated the Field Integrated Innovation Accelerator, a business development program for co-innovation and co-economic development teams. As the program grew, we extended our reach, developing relationships with the US Agency for International Development (USAID) as they considered funding projects that improved regional win-win economics. But with success came the end of the three-year run and a time-sensitive need to recalibrate.

We gathered for another three-day session in Seattle to consider the next steps. The Integrated Business Roundtable (IBR) had a proof of concept, and it was time to develop a new plan for future growth.

We went back to our values. With all its moving parts, one of the most rewarding and meaningful outcomes of the three-year process had been the fact that a group of Christians from across the United States could collaborate and effectively invest in Israeli technologies. The emergent consensus was to focus on the value of Christian economic partnership with Israeli technology.

Mike Humphrey led the charge, establishing Fieron Growth Partners with our friend and associate, John Handelsman. Mike and John merged their venture capital and equity finance practices to provide growth capital and generate measurable social impact. The new fund isn't limited to investments in Israel, but the region promises to become a significant part of their portfolio.

The other values, those that weren't the focus of the new plan, live on. Some have found new homes in different organizations. Some, like the Israeli-Palestinian Business Integration, are always in flux, both before and after the current Hamas-Israel war. But not every value can or should be part of every plan.

Recalibrating can be challenging. When doing so with a team, it may require some hard conversations. Deciding between which values to prioritize, which causes to invest in, or the size and scope of a budget, is a trying process. But the reward is well worth the effort.

Refinement is a critical aspect of our Kosher Giving Plan. It's important to avoid the comfort of simply repeating last year's strategies. As we recognize the completion of certain processes, it opens the door to reassess and redirect our resources. This evolution in our approach is not just about change for its own sake, but a thoughtful realignment, ensuring our resources are applied where they are currently most needed, maintaining a coherent and impactful role throughout our philanthropic journey.

Kosher Food for Thought

What's your approach to refining your Kosher Giving Plan? After revisiting your Kosher Giving Plan, what aspect of your implementation are you most motivated to refine or develop further?

How did the refinement process affect your giving decisions? In reassessing your budget, what new priorities have emerged, and how do they align with your values?

Are you happy with the result? Thinking about the operational efficiency of your giving, what areas do you see as opportunities for improvement?

Kosher Giving Applied Actions

1. Use your Kosher Giving Journal to record your answers to the Kosher Food for Thought above.
2. Use your Kosher Giving Plan Workbook to track your conclusions and refine your Plan for the next giving season.
3. Open a new Worksheet within your Workbook to begin designing next season's Plan.

Part 4: Supercharge Your Giving

Chapter Twelve

Partners in Philanthropy

Beyond the basics of kosher giving, there are opportunities to supercharge meaningful, mindful, and measurable philanthropy. By now, we've discovered the pillars of needs, impact agents and purpose that form the backbone of our plan. We've studied the four steps of design, implementation, evaluation, and refinement. But there's one more ingredient to our Kosher Giving Plan that requires our thoughtful attention. It's the unifying piece that brings everything together: our partners.

One of the most overused and abused terms in philanthropy is 'partnership.' We're often asked to partner with a cause or a program, so much so that the term 'partner' begins to lose its meaning. But the term *is* meaningful (which is precisely why it's so overused).

In philanthropy, partners vary in their roles and contributions. A partner could be your spouse, collaborating to craft and execute your Kosher Giving Plan. Alternatively, it could be a child or grandchild, offering new perspectives and aiding in creating a legacy of intergenerational impact. A partner might also be a trusted friend, mentor, or protégé, whose insights and advice you value. It could be another philanthropist who you choose to work with in contributing to multiple projects. Additionally, professionals with domain expertise can be partners, guiding you through the complexities of the philanthropic landscape and assisting you through comprehensive planning and execution.

Our partners in philanthropy are the people who join us for the journey. Your giving partners may not accompany you in every situation, but they're people who you turn to advance certain values or promote certain causes. And as tried-and-true partners, they're people with whom you often develop two-way relationships, through which a partnership project initiated by one of the parties is often reciprocated by an invitation from the other party to join their initiative.

Trusted, dependable partners, who complement your efforts with an evolving set of win-wins, have the capacity to further infuse the kosher giving principles with additional meaning and mindfulness. By harnessing effective planning and execution, they can multiply the effects of your purpose, impact agents, and outcomes. And through sustained relationships, you're likely to find yourself partnering with some of the same select people, time and time again
.

Investing in Relationships

A Tractate in Pirkei Avot (lit. Chapters of the Fathers) makes a puzzling statement:

> "Joshua ben Perahiah used to say: appoint for thyself a mentor, and acquire for thyself a companion..."
> **Pirkei Avot 1:6**

Unclear as "*appoint for thyself a mentor*" may be, as we generally don't get to appoint our teachers, the call to "*acquire for thyself a companion*" seems even less understood. The Hebrew word, " *k'neh*," translated here as "*acquire,*" is more commonly translated as purchase. The term "*chaver*" (pronounced khah-vër) can mean a friend, a person of community status, or a companion. Are we expected to acquire or purchase companions and friends? Aren't those relationships expected to be more organic, natural and - perhaps - incidental? And why "companion," in the singular? Why not companions? Shouldn't we value having many friends?

Yes, naturally occurring relationships are a healthy part of everyday life, but there are some domains of life that demand more. Just as we're invited to enlist mentors to educate us, we have much to gain when we invest in a companion. This is particularly true in the context of philanthropic companionship, where our successful planning and execution can resonate beautifully with our core sense of purpose.

Some impact agents act strictly in an advisory capacity as discussed in Chapter 4. However, with others the relationship can be one where not only expertise and information is provided, but the advisor is able to also see through to our values and purpose to assist us in ensuring a complete alignment of our vision and values with an efficient use of our resources and time.

Companions are those advisors who engage more deeply with your vision and values. They may be long-term consultants offering strategic guidance, helping shape your overall approach to giving, and ensuring alignment with your purpose. Their role goes beyond providing a service, as they invest time in understanding you and your aspirations.

To be sure, a legal expert can be a trusted companion, and a long-term consultant may be an on-demand service provider. The distinction is not based upon the services provided or even the length of the engagement. The defining characteristics of a partner or a companion is in the nature of the relationship itself.

Your Philanthropy Companion Checklist

When considering companions for your philanthropic journey, certain baseline qualities are essential:

__ **Trust and honesty:** This one's a deal-breaker. Trust is built over time, but if it doesn't develop or if it's undermined, the relationship simply will not grow.

__ **Shared goals:** Partnerships are not designed to be transactional. You and your professional companion should be working in unison to genuinely advance the same goals.

__ **Respect and understanding:** Just because you hire a professional doesn't mean that you've outsourced your thinking, wisdom, experience, and insight. Your relationship should be marked by a mutual respect, where each party seeks, understands, and appreciates the other's perspectives and expertise.

__ **Transparency:** This differs from trust, but is no less important. Clear communication about strategies, decisions, and work process expectations is essential.

__ **Availability:** A professional partner should be accessible when you need them, demonstrating commitment to your priorities. That doesn't mean that they're waiting by the phone for your next thought or idea, but it does mean that they will prioritize your needs.

These are, as noted, baseline expectations. You hope that every service provider will conduct themselves accordingly, but you most certainly should expect this of your trusted companion.

Navigating the Evolution of Partnerships

I would humbly suggest that truly meaningful and rewarding partnerships have the potential to evolve, beyond their initial context. This evolution can lead to partnerships that outlast the specific projects or engagements that initiated them.

When Mayor Eli Shaviro envisioned a Young Adults Center in Ariel, the late Larry Field took interest. His family foundation had already funded the Lawrence N. Field Center for Entrepreneurship at his alma mater, Baruch College City University of New York. A similar project, operating out of a Young Adults Center and enriched with years of experience from an older sister program across the Atlantic, was poised to become a meaningful contribution to Ariel, its residents, and the region.

The vision was there, but someone needed to make it come to fruition. Lisa Field, who had been assuming an increasingly active role at the Field Family Foundation, took the lead. She knew the Field Center in New York well and saw the potential for a similar program in Ariel.

At the time, I was running the Ariel Development Fund, entrusted with resource development and program oversight for civic initiatives across the city. As those who worked with me can attest, this project quickly became one of my top priorities. I had recently completed my MBA studies, and I was excited to apply some of what I had learned to a philanthropic endeavor that would support the business community.

Lisa and I began with the basics, defining everything from vision and mission to goals and objectives. We refined target audiences, engaged additional stakeholders, and built a giving plan. Lisa cared enough to make the program work, and she remained attuned to developments throughout the six-year implementation process.

Roughly halfway through the project's lifecycle, I made a career shift, moving from the Ariel Development Fund to my work with the Integrated Business Roundtable. The Field Center remained a personal commitment for me, as did my partnership with Lisa. In the following years, I continued to participate in follow-up calls with Lisa and assist in guiding the Field Center for Entrepreneurship at Ariel to meet their objectives, despite having no official role or position. I didn't consider myself a volunteer or a consultant. Lisa and I were philanthropic partners, pursuing the continued success of a project that was meaningful to us both.

It's no wonder, then, that when I reached out to Lisa about a new opportunity, she responded with a resounding "yes."

The Israel Innovation Authority had announced a bid for establishing new technology innovation centers across Israel's periphery. Alongside our kosher giving services and support for the giving community, my advisory firm, Sector4 Strategy, offers services to promote the 'fourth sector'. This is what's often used to refer to the meeting point where government, the private sector and nonprofits all converge to generate greater impact.

We set up a joint venture with businesses, professionals, non-profits, and investors to submit a proposal. When looking for additional funding to make our bid's business plan more robust, Lisa raised her hand.

As I write these pages, we still don't know what the results of this bid will be. The interviews with the Israel Innovation Authority were postponed "until further notice," as the war rages on and national government financing for new initiatives is shifting. But regardless of whether this pans out, Lisa and I remain social impact partners. If it's not this initiative, it will be the next one.

In the case of the Field Center for Entrepreneurship, a sustained partnership persisted beyond changing circumstances and found expression in a new initiative that was aligned with its predecessor. But there are other times when philanthropy partnerships can evolve and thrive in completely new directions with new causes and, to a degree, new values.

The National Leadership Center, which we discussed in Chapter 9 when addressing the implementation step of the Kosher Giving Plan, is one such example. While working on the program's strategic development with Heather Johnston, a spin-off began to take form. It was an entirely new initiative with the same founder and the same commitment to impactful success.

Heather had begun inviting US Congresspeople to travel to Israel to visit the National Leadership Center. They were curious to get a close-up of what an Israeli, Jewish version of JH Ranch looked like, and they were pleased to accept the well-intentioned invitation. But the NLC is in Ariel, and the enthusiastic would-be visitors were not permitted to travel over the Green Line into Judea and Samaria (the West Bank).

This didn't sit well with Heather. First, the NLC is an apolitical education site. Second, if it's a political issue, then why shouldn't congress be visiting a contested region, a region with direct relevance to some of the legislation that they vote on?

For Heather, this was one part injustice, and one part short-sighted policy. Instead of walking away, like everyone else who tried to overcome these challenges in the past, she established the US Israel Education Association, a new nonprofit organization dedicated to educating the US Congress about pressing Israel-related issues. And yes, for more than a decade the organization has been hosting Congressional Ethics Committee approved delegations to Judea and Samaria, year in and year out.

I had the honor of joining the founding board of directors of USIEA. I've hosted their delegations to the region since the organization's birth and thereafter. Heather and I have briefed Congresspeople in Israel and on Capitol Hill. We worked with the White House to arrange the Palestinian delegation to the Peace to Prosperity Workshop in Bahrain, a precursor to the Abraham Accords. And we continue to formulate and clarify current issues for policymakers and media networks. The educational initiative for Israel persists. An educational framework for Congress has evolved. And it's safe to assume that there's more to come.

It seemed only natural to me that I invite Heather to join the Advisory Board of KosherGiving.com. It's true - she has extensive experience with visionary philanthropy, and a thorough appreciation for the value proposition of 'kosher' as a universal set of principles. But there are many people who fit those categories. When I invited Heather to join our board, she accepted, reflecting on the same underlying reasons that prompted me to accept her invitation to join USIEA. We're social impact partners, and partners continue to work together, especially when there's lots of good to be done.

Long-term, strategic partnerships with professional advisors aren't a given, nor are they always essential. Typically, the journey starts with building trust, one program at a time. In some cases, with experience, this professional relationship may grow into a lasting and meaningful philanthropy partnership. It's not the objective, but it is possible.

At Sector4 Strategy, we provide clearly defined advisory services to our clients. The relationship is well-defined, predicated upon the trust, transparency, respect, and availability described earlier.

When working on an organizational scale-up, a Kosher Giving Plan, or a comprehensive inter-sector economic initiative, Sector4 engagements are goal-oriented and outcome-tested.

Recognizing the potential for lasting partnerships that may follow project-based engagements adds depth to the work process.

Partnerships in philanthropy *are* meaningful. Once you've come this far on your philanthropic journey, consider investing in a companion.

The Right Time for Partnership and a Companion

Are you the sort of person who pursues professional advisors and consultants, or do you prefer the do-it-yourself approach?

Your Kosher Giving Plan is best designed and executed with the help of an experienced professional, but with the right time, effort, and commitment, you can use this book to guide you on an effective and meaningful kosher giving journey on your own.

There are, however, some situations where the complexity of your giving plan changes over the course of your refinement process, and the breadth of your ambitions calls for professional guidance. Here are some telltale signs that it's probably time to "*acquire a companion*":

Your giving plan became more complex: As your aspirations in philanthropy grow, so does the need for sophisticated strategies. A professional advisor can offer the expertise required to navigate challenges related to your giving plan becoming more complex.

You're battling time constraints: Balancing philanthropy with other responsibilities can become time-consuming. If managing your giving plan starts to overwhelm your schedule, it's a sign that you could benefit from the support of a professional.

You seek to make a broader impact: If you're looking to scale your philanthropic impact or give to new causes in new fields, a professional partner can provide insights and access to networks and opportunities beyond your current scope.

You desire strategic growth: When you aspire to evolve from spontaneous giving to a more strategic approach, a professional can guide this transition, ensuring that your philanthropic efforts align with your values and long-term vision.

Kosher Food for Thought

Who are your trusted philanthropy partners as of today? Friends? Impact agents? Family Advisors?

Consider the qualities you value in a professional advisor. Which of these qualities are most prominent in the people you work with?

Have you ever strategically shifted your philanthropy? Under which circumstances might you choose to seek professional assistance?

Kosher Giving Applied Actions

1. Use your Kosher Giving Journal to record your answers to the Kosher Food for Thought above.

2. List the advisors, consultants, and coaches whom you've worked with, whether in the field of business, personal development, recreation or otherwise. Note how many of those have assisted you with philanthropy. Set and record a goal for either changing or maintaining a philanthropy partnership with a trusted professional.

3. If you seek a new professional philanthropy advisor, reach out to Sector4 Strategy at www.sector4.xyz or contact another service provider with a proven track record.

Chapter Thirteen

Shalom Giving

A book about giving that doesn't address Shalom would be tragically incomplete.

'Kosher' is an excellent way to frame giving. It makes us mindful about our donations, aware of the why, how, what and who behind our philanthropy. It provides a point of departure, rooted in Jewish heritage and extending to all families on earth. Kosher is a good start, but it's nowhere near the limit of what your giving can achieve.

In this book, we've explored the mutual impact of philanthropy, discussing how our giving benefits others and enriches us. We've considered our values, roles, and purpose, viewing philanthropy as both a means to an end and an end in and of itself. We've recognized that the philanthropy chain—encompassing the giver, the impact agent, and the recipient—creates mutual benefits for all involved.

Kosher giving, at its essence, is about fostering positive and meaningful interactions between individuals and their environments. It's about looking beyond oneself and enriching the world with personal contributions. When you embrace kosher giving, you're consciously and thoughtfully impacting the world around you.

Yet, this raises a question: what about those who haven't yet engaged in kosher giving? How do we encourage and inspire them to participate in this fulfilling and impactful approach to philanthropy?

We began our kosher giving journey speaking about war. The ongoing war has colored everything that I have personally experienced while writing this book. It has directly caused tectonic shifts in Israel-focused philanthropy and serves as a compelling case study for us to learn about giving under extreme circumstances. After all, if we can respond effectively to the extreme, then we can manage the normative.

Whatever the circumstances, giving is about tending to something that's broken. In war, there is no shortage of things that are broken. Possessions, Homes. Families. Lives. Health. Stability. Hope. War is painful, not only because of what's already broken, but out of concern that things might get worse before they get better. But what happens when there are no wars? When there's a ceasefire? When the land is quiet? There's still so much that's broken, and so much that needs to be fixed.

A Shalom Paradigm

We do ourselves a disservice when we confuse two very different words: peace and tranquility. Tranquility is a lack of disturbance and a calm, almost motionless state of silence. Israel's peace treaties with Egypt and with Jordan are often referred to as 'cold peace'. The treaties have yielded a lack of war. They've brought relative tranquility. But they're not truly about peace. 'Cold peace' isn't peace at all.

In Israel, the word "*shalom*" has multiple meanings: hello, goodbye, and peace.

The root of shalom is *shalem*, or complete, whole.

Shalom is not about an empty silence, but rather a powerful harmony. Shalom is what happens when all the different voices sing together, when all the moving parts come together like clockwork.

Shalom is the sum of all positive forces, each at full volume, yet giving each other the space they need to express themselves well.

If kosher giving is about an individual's impact, then shalom giving is about the impact that the collective can generate. It's what happens when everyone is doing their part, giving what they can, and providing the space for everyone else to do the same.

The stats suggest that Joseph Gitler of Leket Israel is right. If we can rescue enough food that's already available, then there will be enough for everyone to be able to eat. Tali Tabib of Alumot B'Omer is also right. If we boldly reassess what our role is, even-or perhaps especially in times of crisis then the bereaved families who need us most will receive a warm, healing embrace. Gal Barzilay of Hightech4Israel is right as well. If we learn from our failures and focus on our G-d-given and experience-enhanced talents, we can tackle the problems that no one else seems to be capable of handling.

Kosher giving is our modest, genuine commitment to move the needle on a world filled with seemingly endless needs. And even if shalom giving is beyond our reach as individuals, every person who joins the kosher giving community brings us one voice closer to a pitch-perfect, peaceful harmony.

Kosher Food for Thought

Let's address community engagement. Have you ever given as part of a group? Did the experience allow you to find or better your purpose?

When has your giving been more impactful than you had originally anticipated? Have you taken an interest in collaborating with other funders?

Can you envision shalom? If everyone was contributing to every need in the most appropriate way, what would that look like for you? Would you be applying more effort to your giving, or less?

Kosher Giving Applied Actions

1. Use your Kosher Giving Journal to record your answers to the Kosher Food for Thought above.
2. Make a list of five funders with whom you'd like to collaborate to benefit a cause. Set a goal to invite one of them to join you on one cause within a set timeframe. Record in your journal.
3. Go to https://www.koshergiving.com/community. Discover the opportunity to join a community of like-minded philanthropists who want to give better through mutual experiences and collaborative growth.

Chapter Fourteen

What's Next?

There's no need to wait. You have everything you need to embark on your philanthropic journey in the pages of this book.

> **You know why you give—because it's an integral part of who you are.**

You're familiar with various approaches to giving, each valuable, with some being more effective than others.

So, if you haven't done so yet, start by reflecting on the three pillars of kosher giving outlined above. Make good use of your understanding of how to assess needs, collaborate with impact agents, and discover a personal purpose in your philanthropic endeavors. These steps are not simple, but they can't be overlooked either. Take the necessary time to grasp these fundamentals before proceeding with your Kosher Giving Plan.

Armed with the basics, it's time to make a commitment. You don't want a series of disjointed lists of pillars and values. You want this to become a cohesive unit, a meaningful action plan, and a step towards shalom. Reflect, choose with intention, and commit to the rewarding work process that will follow.

Then, engage with the four steps of your Kosher Giving Plan: design, implement, evaluate, and refine. Revisit these steps as needed, engaging with the questions at the end of each chapter, and utilizing the accompanying Kosher Giving Journal and Kosher Giving Plan Workbook. This process is cyclical—design your plan, move towards implementation, evaluate, and refine. And when the cycle is complete and you've come to appreciate how the process has impacted you and those around you, refine.

And finally, take a close look at who you invite to join you on your journey. Kosher giving is, by definition, about reaching beyond oneself. It's both deeply personal and fundamentally a shared process. Find a trustworthy companion, be it friend, family or professional and invest in that relationship, so that your kosher giving can reach its full potential.

There's so much to do, and so much that you can accomplish. As we sign off with a prayer for peace, know that the Sector4 Strategy and KosherGiving.com teams are here with and for you, striving to serve those driven by purpose. We thank you for stepping up, filling the void, and continually refining your kosher giving craft. We wish you effective impact and blessings in your endeavors.

Shalom.

Kosher Food for Thought

What is your giving purpose? Who were you before your kosher giving journey? Who are you now?

What are your impact goals? When all is said and done, how will you move the needle to make the world a better place?

How would you articulate the case of better giving to others? By becoming a better giver, you can consider how you give the gift of better giving.

Kosher Giving Applied Actions

1. Use your Kosher Giving Journal to record your answers to the Kosher Food for Thought above.

2. Generate more shalom giving by gifting copies of this book to two like-minded friends or family members.

3. Keep your copy of this book close by as a point of reference throughout the design, implementation, evaluation, and refinement of next season's Kosher Giving Plan.

Kosher Giving Resources

Download the FREE Kosher Giving Journal and Workbook to track your Kosher Giving journey and build your plan at KosherGiving.com/tools

Download book supplements, including the Kosher Giving Action Plan video series, workshops, and additional content at KosherGiving.com/book.

Join the Kosher Giving Society: KosherGiving.com/community.

Schedule an appointment for a consultation with Avi or a Sector4 Strategy advisor at KosherGiving.com.

Interview Avi or bring him in to speak. Reach out to him and his team at KosherGiving.com/book.

Sign up for our newsletter to receive donor tools, giving opportunities, invitations to webinars, and more at KosherGiving.com.

Follow us on social media:
https://www.instagram.com/koshergiving/
https://www.linkedin.com/company/sector4-strategy-ltd

Frequently Asked Questions

1. I'm not Jewish and I don't keep kosher. What can Kosher Giving offer me?

Kosher Giving is for everyone who wants to give. It's not limited to or focused on religious dietary practices. It's a universal approach focused on impactful and mindful philanthropy. Regardless of your background, this framework offers valuable insights into making your giving more meaningful and effective.

2. I wouldn't consider myself a 'philanthropist' but I do like to give. Is this book for me?

Absolutely! Kosher Giving is for anyone interested in making their contributions more purposeful, whether you give a little or a lot. It's about the quality and thoughtfulness of your giving, not the quantity.

3. I already have a Donor Advised Fund or a family foundation. Why should I read this book?

This book will provide you with strategies to enhance the impact of your Donor Advised Fund or family Foundation. It offers tools to align your giving with your values and making informed decisions about where and how to contribute.

4. The Kosher Giving Plan seems very time-consuming. Is there an easier approach to kosher giving?

While the Kosher Giving Plan is comprehensive, individuals can apply the principles of kosher giving in flexible ways. Download the Kosher Giving Journal and the Kosher Giving Plan Workbook to track your progress and focus on the areas that are most important to you.

5. I'd like to get to work immediately. How can I connect with an advisor?

To connect with a Kosher Giving advisor, you can visit our website at KosherGiving.com or email the Sector4 Strategy team directly at info@sector4.xyz. We'll guide you to a suitable advisor who's aligned with your philanthropic goals.

About the Author

Avi Zimmerman is a social and business entrepreneur, dedicated to generating lasting impact through thoughtful partnerships.

At the beginning of the Hamas-Israel Iron Swords War in October 2023, Avi identified a surge in civilian needs, an influx of donations, and misalignment between the two. He launched Kosher Giving.com and wrote the Kosher Giving book with the goal of providing funders with the tools to give better.

The Founder and CEO of Sector4 Strategy, an Israel-based advisory firm, Avi has extensive experience in diplomacy, project development, and innovation mentoring. He is a sought-after advisor for businesses, non-profits, and government entities.

In recent years, Avi has founded and headed several social and business initiatives. One such initiative is the Judea and Samaria Chamber of Commerce and Industry, established in 2017 to promote a thriving regional economy by creating a network that spans populations, embracing international trade, and promoting synergistic partnerships.

Avi believes that direct and intentional engagement with complex ecosystems can unlock untold opportunities. In 2019, Avi launched the first Israeli-Palestinian Economic Forum, an international conference for inter-population economic development. And in 2020, he co-founded the Integrated Business Roundtable, a group of global impact investors committed to incentivizing inter-population enterprises by sidestepping political landmines and focusing on direct foreign investment. These initiatives follow his decade of service as the Executive Director of the Ariel Development Fund, a foundation that serves the needs of the city he calls home.

Throughout his career, Avi has identified the common fault-lines between the differing cultures of business, nonprofit and government work. With an innovative mindset and a passion for generating positive impact, he began to share his experience-based guidance in multitiered collaborations that benefit diverse communities.

As with Sector4, Avi designed the Kosher Giving project by focusing on his purpose, the needs at hand, and his role in facilitating meaningful impact. Avi formulates his work with like-minded associates, rooted in Torah-inspired social values. Avi studied advanced degrees at Hebrew University and Tel Aviv University and earned his MBA at Ariel University.

When not on speaking tours, Avi prepares carefully packaged personal meals for his five children before they head off to school, and enjoys growing watermelons and grapes on his balcony, anticipating the sweet fruits of his consistent cultivation.

Reach out to Avi at aviz@sector4.xyz or through the website.

You can also connect with him via LinkedIn at
https://www.linkedin.com/in/avi-zimmerman/

Kosher Giving Personal Offer

Congratulations on your completion of the Kosher Giving book! Now, it's time to take action with a special, personal offer.

Visit KosherGiving.com/offer now to unlock your exclusive benefit!

This offer is designed to support you on your path to meaningful, mindful and measurable giving, providing additional tools and resources to enhance your impact. Don't miss this opportunity to deepen your engagement and to make your giving even more effective and fulfilling.

Your Kosher Giving journey doesn't end here. This is a new beginning. Let's continue making a difference, together.

Visit: koshergiving.com/offer

Join The Kosher Giving Community

Congratulations on your completion of the Kosher Giving book! Now, it's time to take action with a special, personal offer.

Your Opportunity

Become a valued member of the Kosher Giving Community. Designed for readers who appreciate the case for "Kosher Giving," this community is a home for those who embrace purposeful and impactful philanthropy.

Discounted Annual Membership: $360 — a 70% savings!

Your Membership Benefits

- Early Access: Be the first to receive digital content, directly resonating with the values and strategies of Kosher Giving.
- Exclusive Discounts: Enjoy reduced rates for upcoming programs and events.
- Contribute to Growth: Your membership helps us further develop KosherGiving.com, a social enterprise plat-

form dedicated to meaningful, mindful and meaningful philanthropy.

Join Today at KosherGiving.com/community.

Make sure to use your special
Kosher Giving reader's **discount code**:

KGREADER

Your journey in better giving continues. This offer is designed to support you on your path to meaningful, mindful and measurable giving, providing additional tools and resources to enhance your impact. Don't miss this opportunity to deepen your engagement and to make your giving even more effective and fulfilling. Join a community that learns, grows and gives with purpose and impact.

Visit KosherGiving.com/community to unlock this exclusive offer.

Available for a limited time only.

A Small Favor

Thank you for taking the time to read Kosher Giving. Every person who reads this book represents a world of untold opportunities.

I hope this journey through the concepts, pillars, phases, and partnerships of Kosher Giving has been meaningful for you.

I'd Love to Hear from You

Your feedback is invaluable. Please consider leaving an honest review of this book, wherever you purchased it. Your insights can help others discover purpose, meaning, and impact through Kosher Giving.

Give the Gift of More Impactful Giving

If you found this book beneficial, please share it with friends, family, and colleagues. The principles of kosher giving can make anyone and everyone a better giver.

Thank you, and best wishes for more meaningful, mindful, and measurable giving,

Avi

Visit us at BeverlyHousePress.com

www.ingramcontent.com/pod-product-compliance
Lightning Source LLC
Chambersburg PA
CBHW061701240326
41458CB00162B/6902/J

* 9 7 8 1 9 5 7 4 6 6 0 6 4 *